# in
# LOVE
# & PAJAMAS

Also by Catana Chetwynd

*Little Moments of Love*
*Snug*

# in
# LOVE
# & PAJAMAS

a collection of comics about being yourself together

## CATANA CHETWYND

**Andrews McMeel**
PUBLISHING®

To two of our biggest fans:
Mama and Papa Chet

## INTRODUCTION

You know that feeling when you're doing something really weird—like dancing around in your pj's with a broomstick to a song that hasn't been popular for seven years—while your partner watches on, and you realize that you don't even have a hint of embarrassment in you? This happens to me often.

First, I think, "*Should* I be embarrassed?"

Then, I think, "Hmm, no. This is me. And I am so lucky to be with someone who not only puts up with this but also embraces it, encourages it."

And my dance moves are *bad* so that's saying something.

Being yourself with your partner—and embracing your partner's quirks—is such an important part of a relationship and is the very foundation for *all* the moments. The silly moments, the quiet moments, the broomstick-dancing moments, and everything in between. No matter who you are, being the truest form of yourself and letting your guard down is what makes all these memories what they are.

This book is for you guys. For all the love you share, all the vulnerability you show, and all the realness you let flow freely. A book for all the moments in love, in pajamas, and, of course, both! We hope you have a comfy spot to sit and a cozy pair of pj's while you open this book and read.

Love,
Catana & John

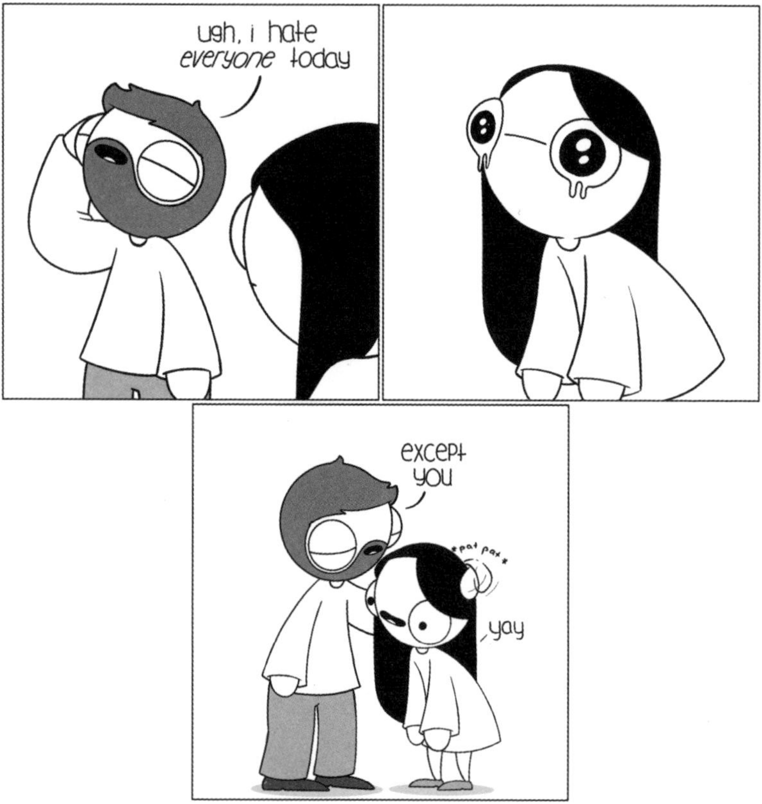
ugh, i hate *everyone* today
except you
*pat pat*
yay

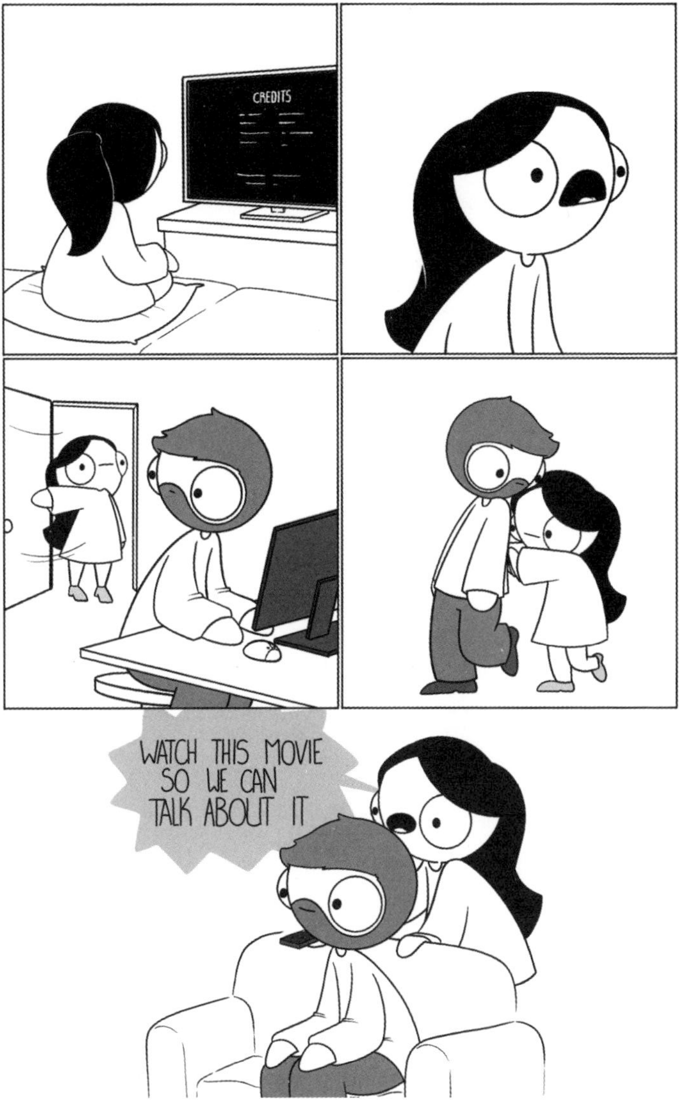
CREDITS
WATCH THIS MOVIE SO WE CAN TALK ABOUT IT

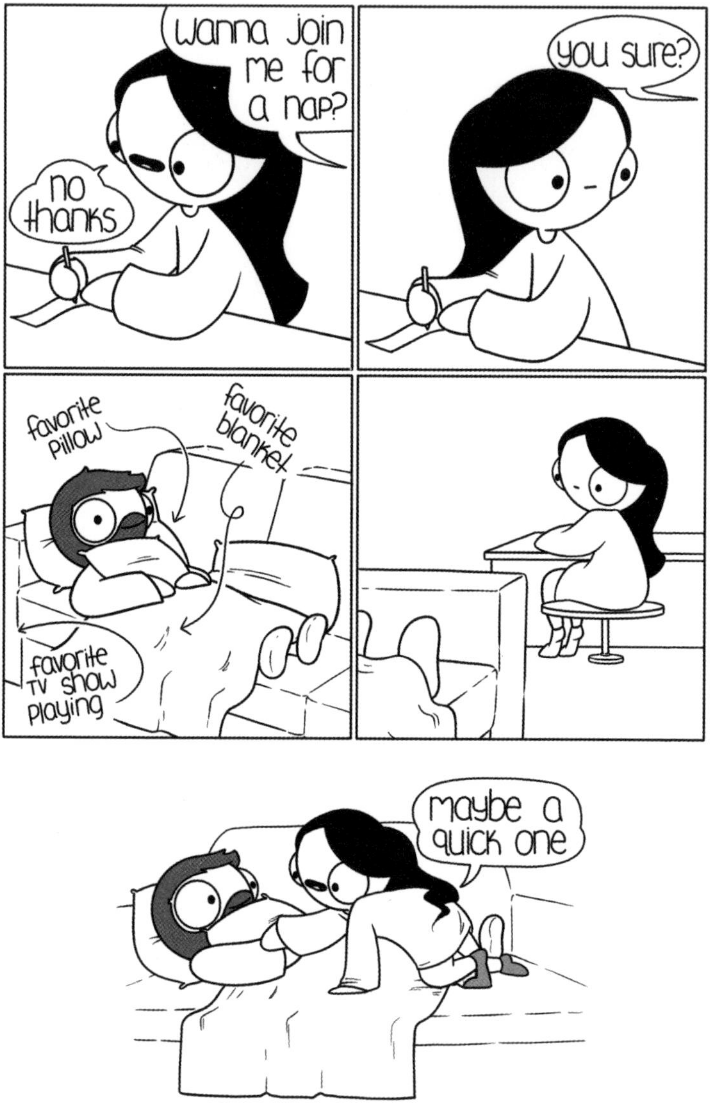
wanna join me for a nap?
no thanks
you sure?
favorite pillow
favorite blanket
favorite TV show playing
maybe a quick one

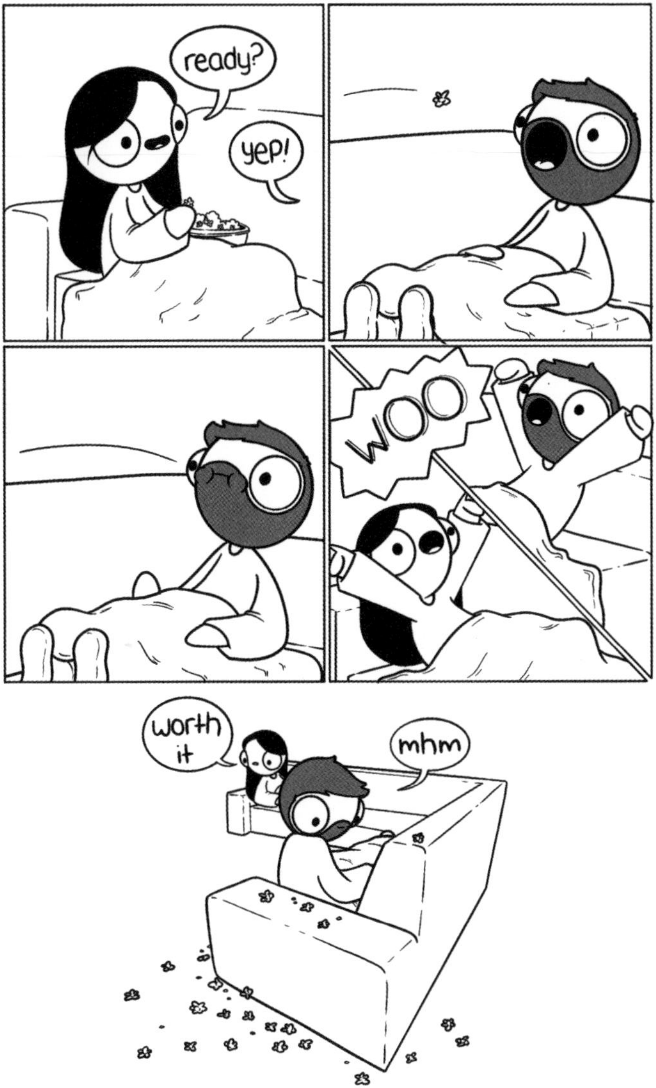
ready?
yep!
WOOO
worth it
mhm

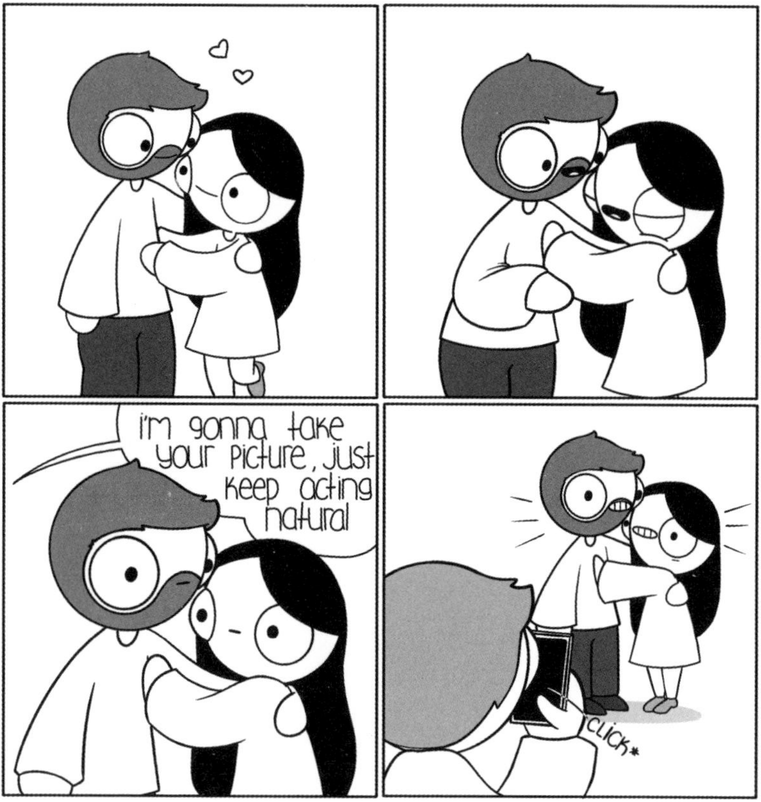
i'm gonna take your picture, just keep acting natural
*CLICK*

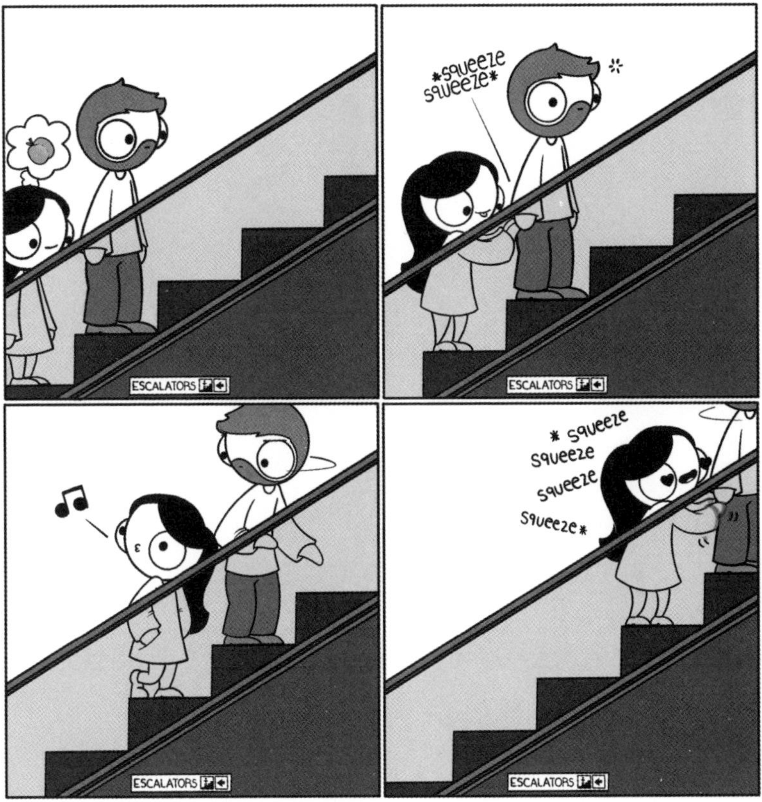
ESCALATORS
*squeeze squeeze*
ESCALATORS
ESCALATORS
* squeeze
squeeze
squeeze
squeeze*
ESCALATORS

# TYPES OF HUGS!

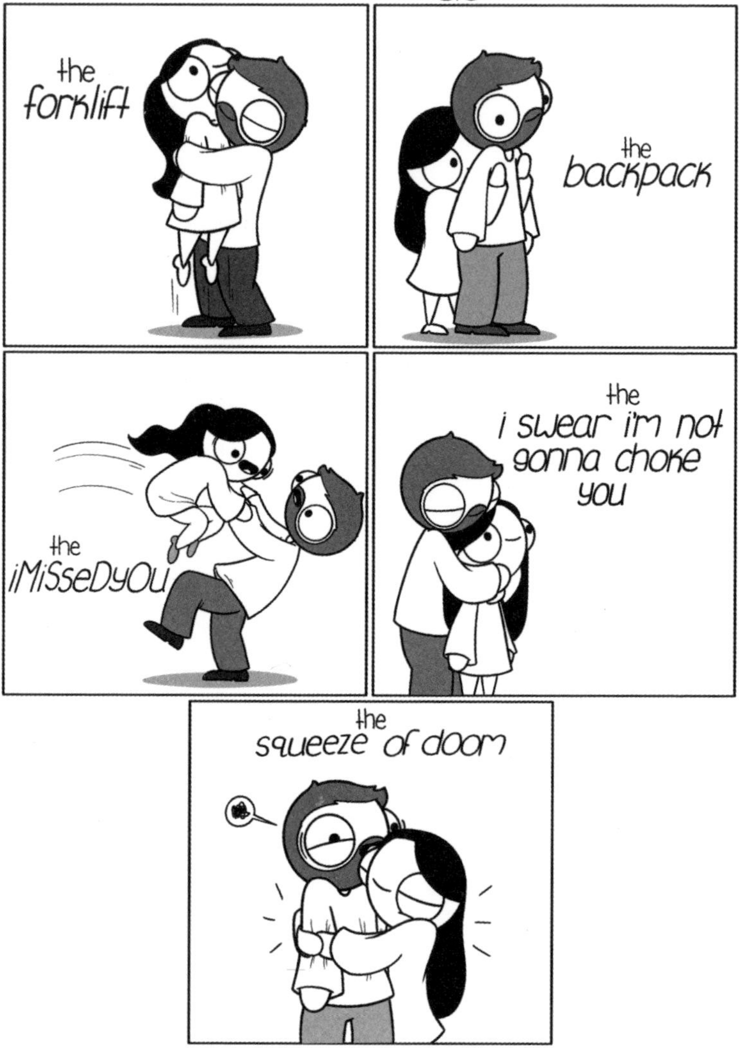
the forklift
the backpack
the iMiSSeDyOu
the i swear i'm not gonna choke you
the squeeze of doom

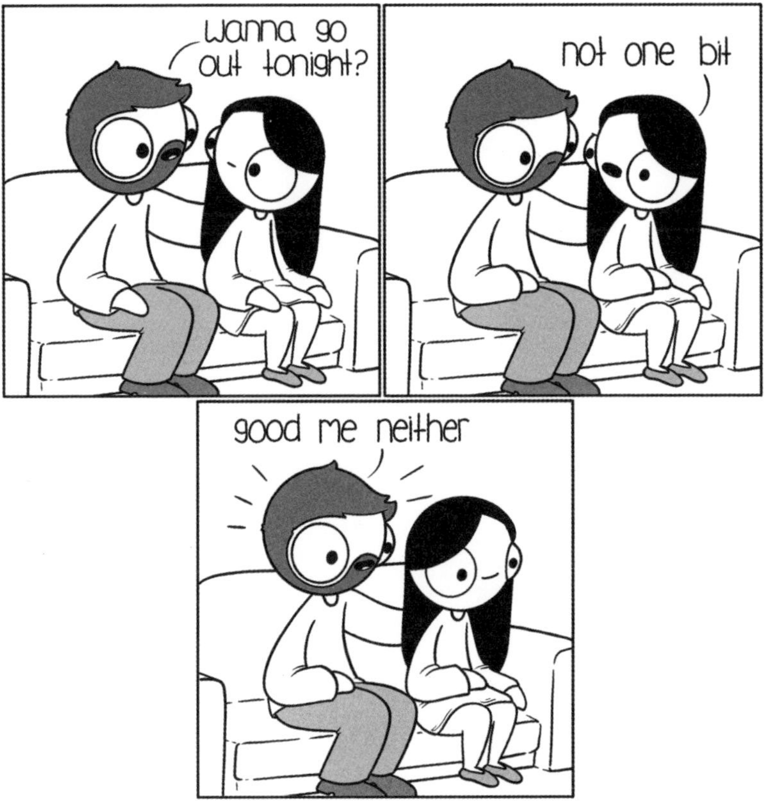
wanna go out tonight?
not one bit
good me neither

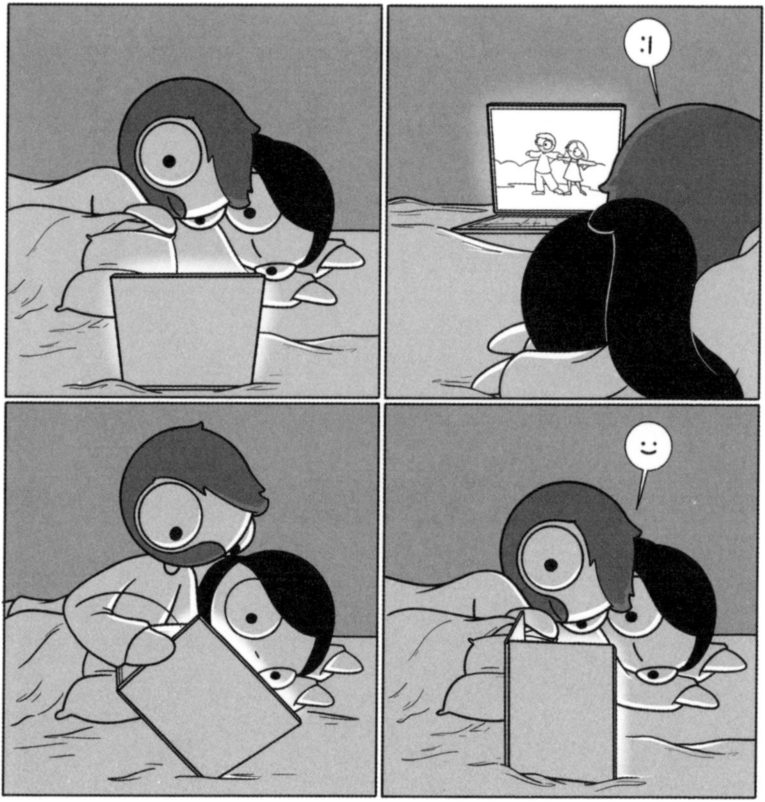

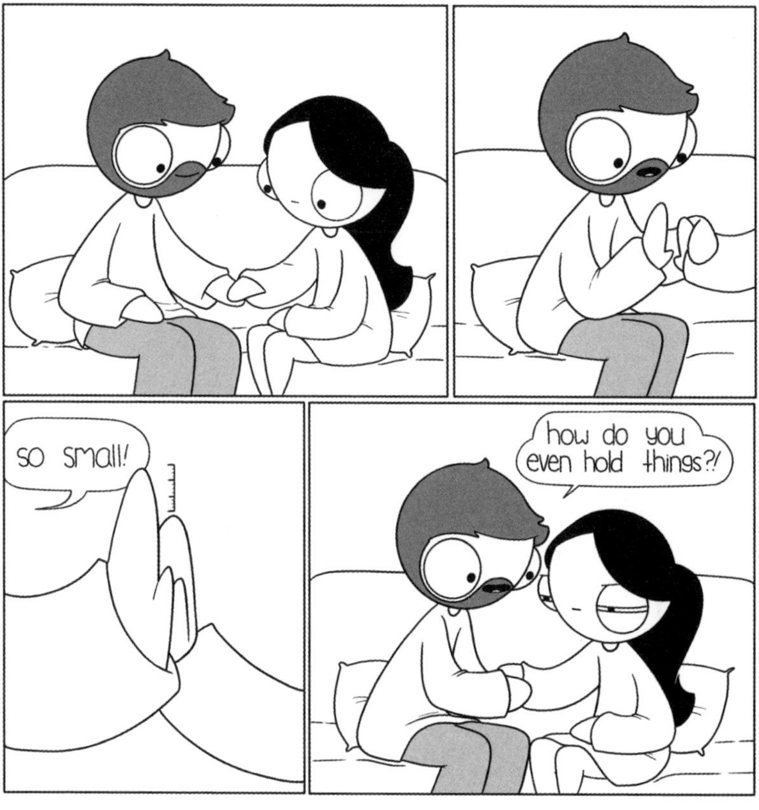
so small!
how do you even hold things?!

what we *should* be like:

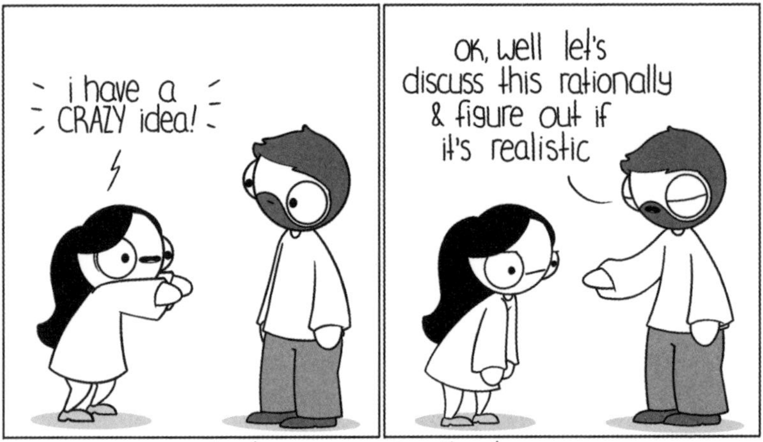
i have a CRAZY idea!
ok, well let's discuss this rationally & figure out if it's realistic

what we're actually like:

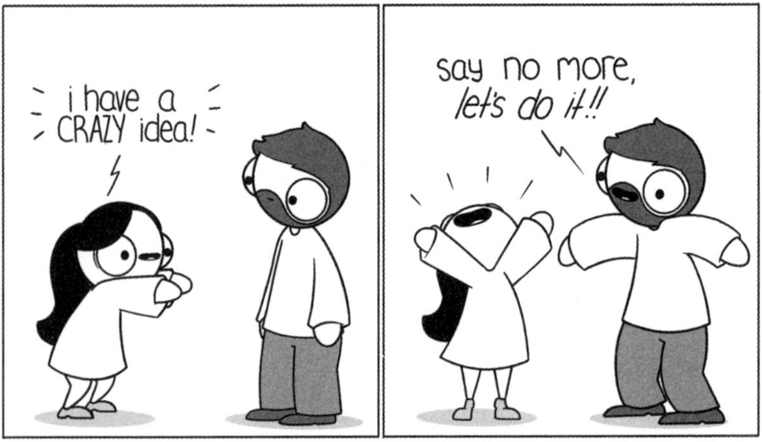
i have a CRAZY idea!
say no more, *let's do it!!*

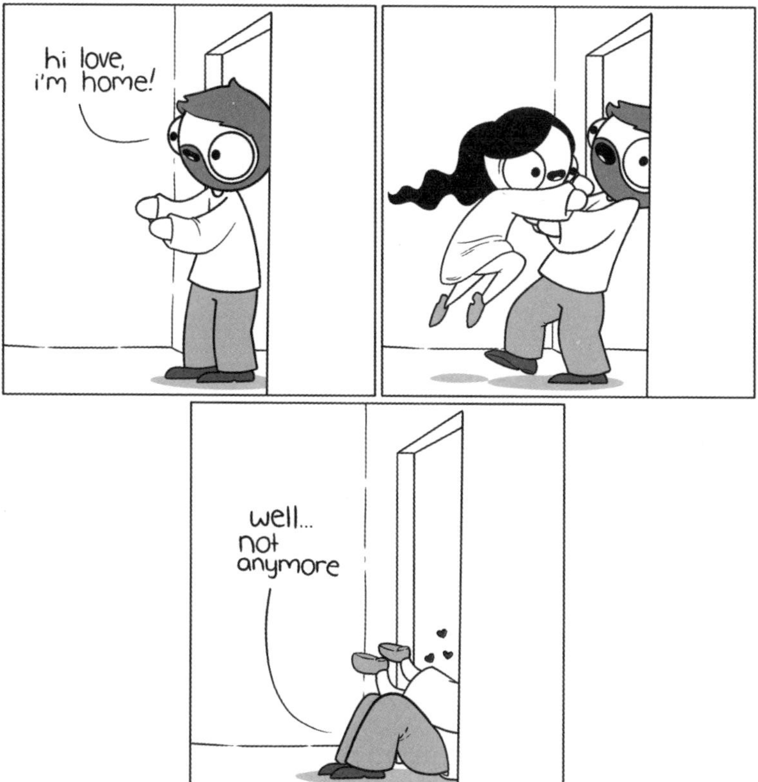
hi love, i'm home!
well... not anymore

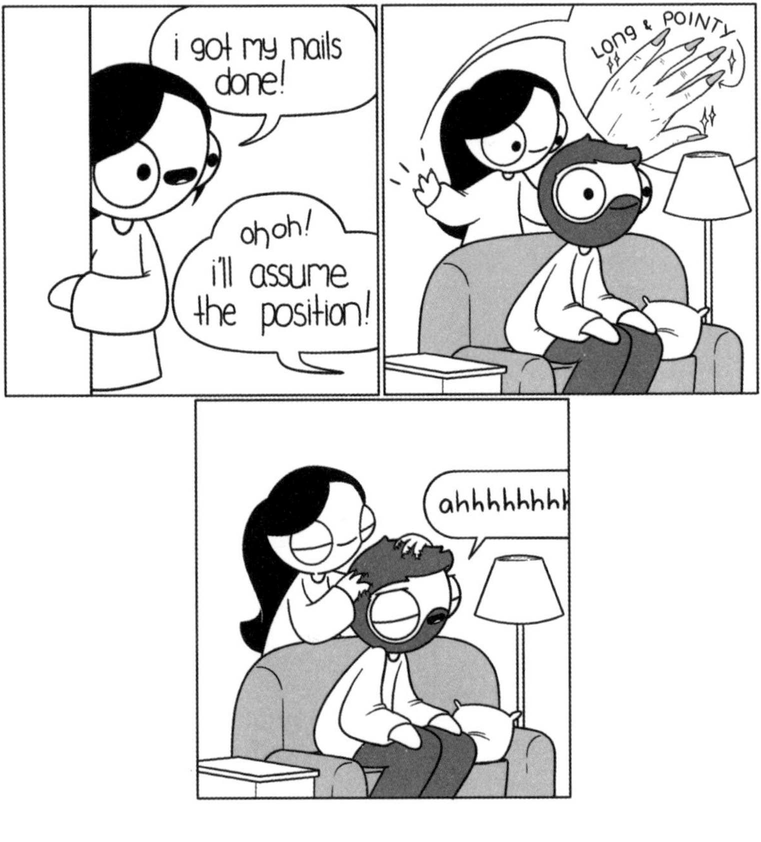
i got my nails done!
ohoh! i'll assume the position!
LONG & POINTY
ahhhhhhhh

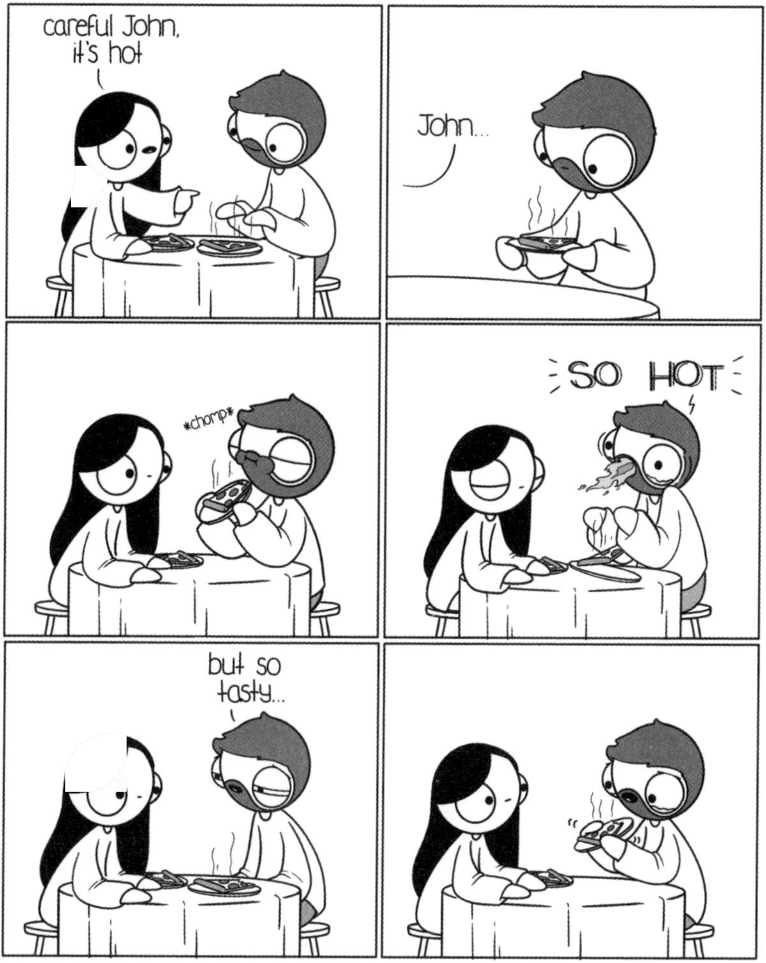
careful John,
it's hot
John...
*chomp*
SO HOT
but so
tasty...

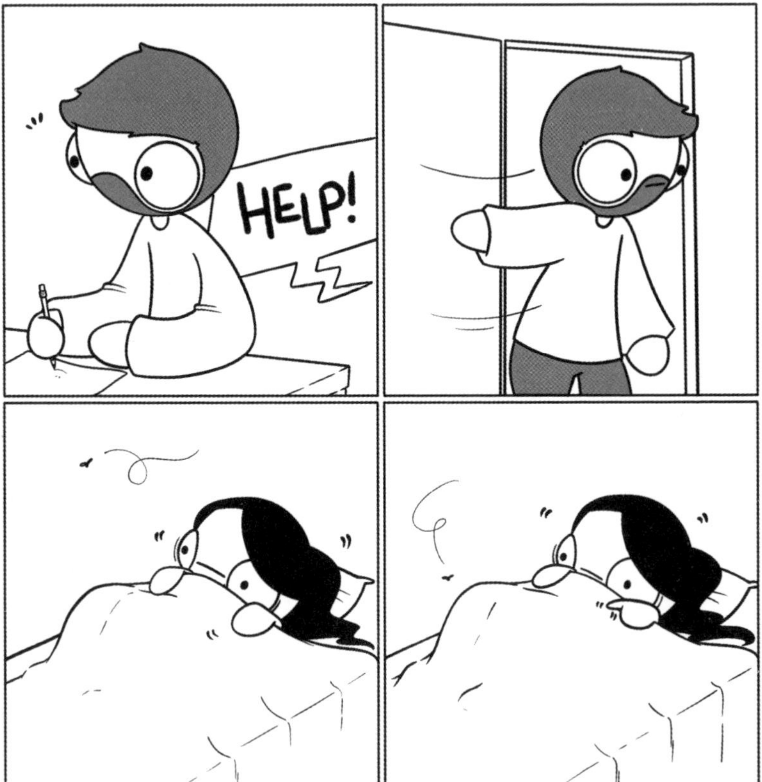
HELP!

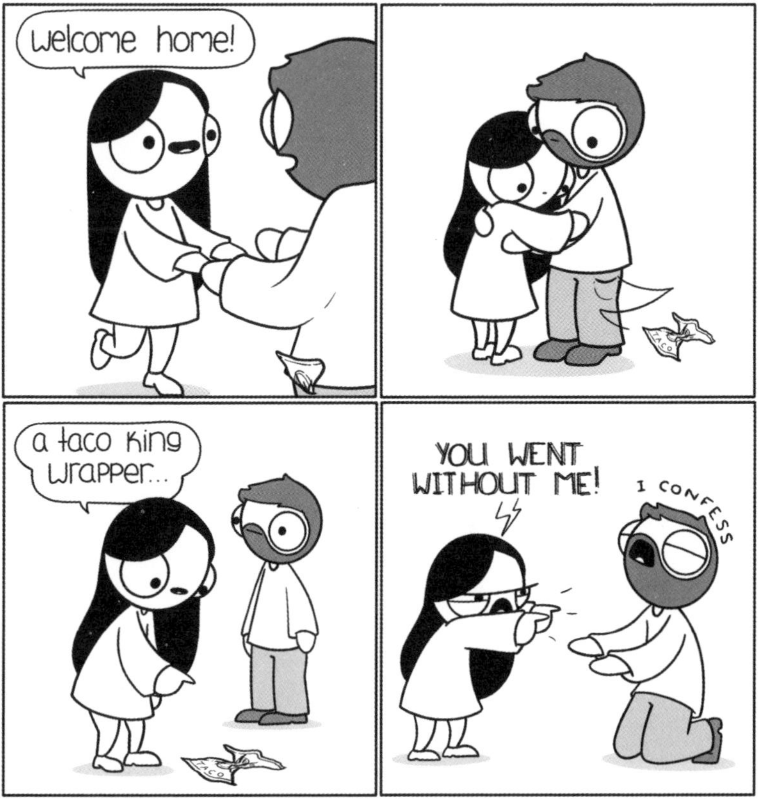
welcome home!
TACO
a taco king wrapper...
TACO
YOU WENT WITHOUT ME!
I CONFESS

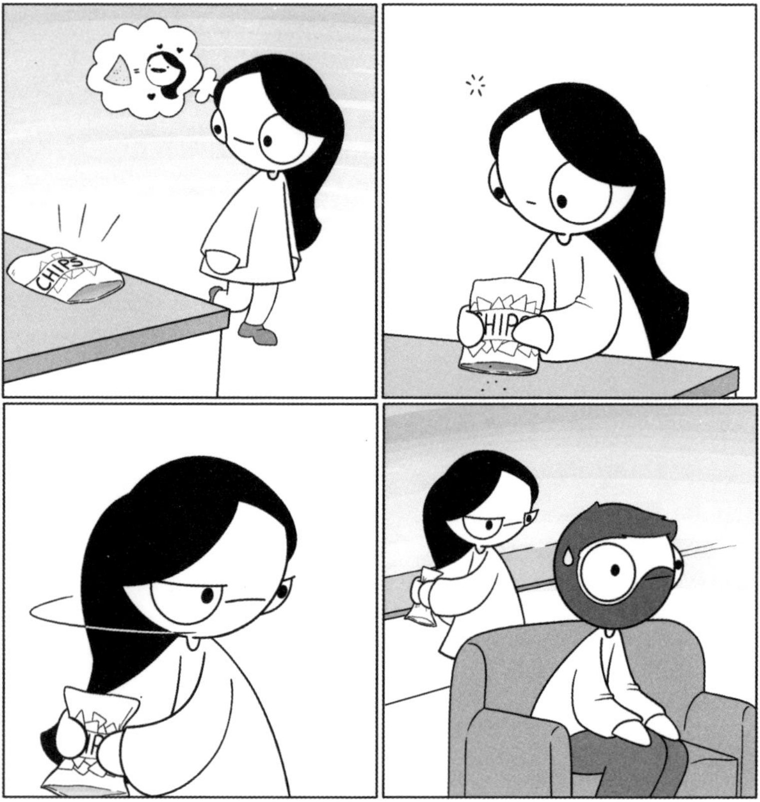
CHIPS

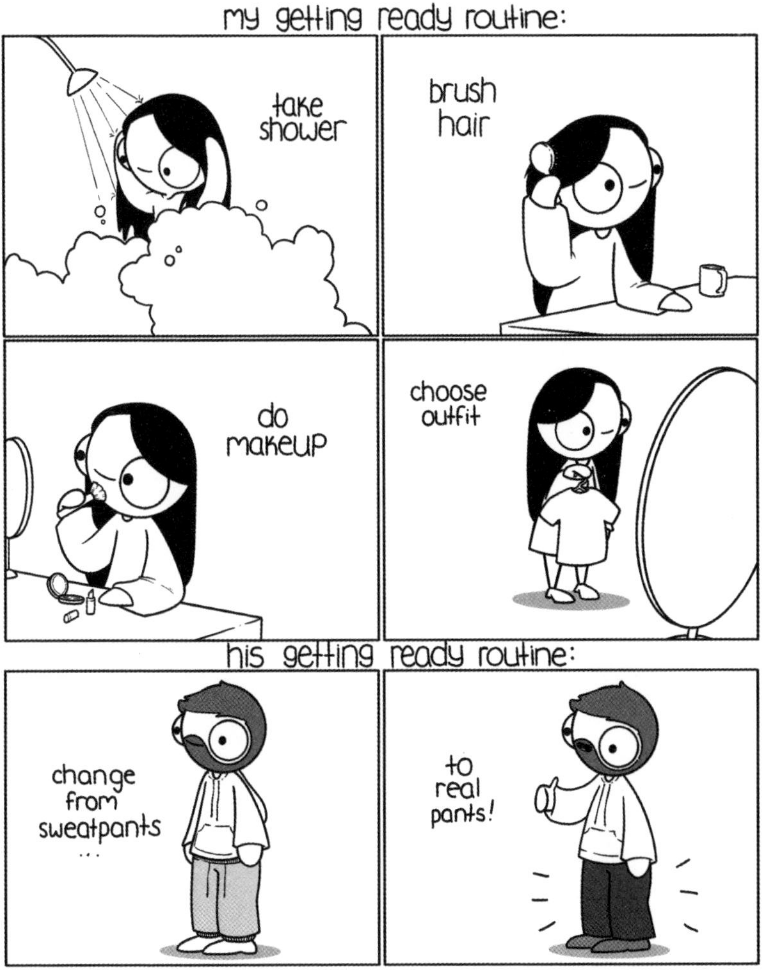
my getting ready routine:
take shower
brush hair
do makeup
choose outfit
his getting ready routine:
change from sweatpants ...
to real pants!

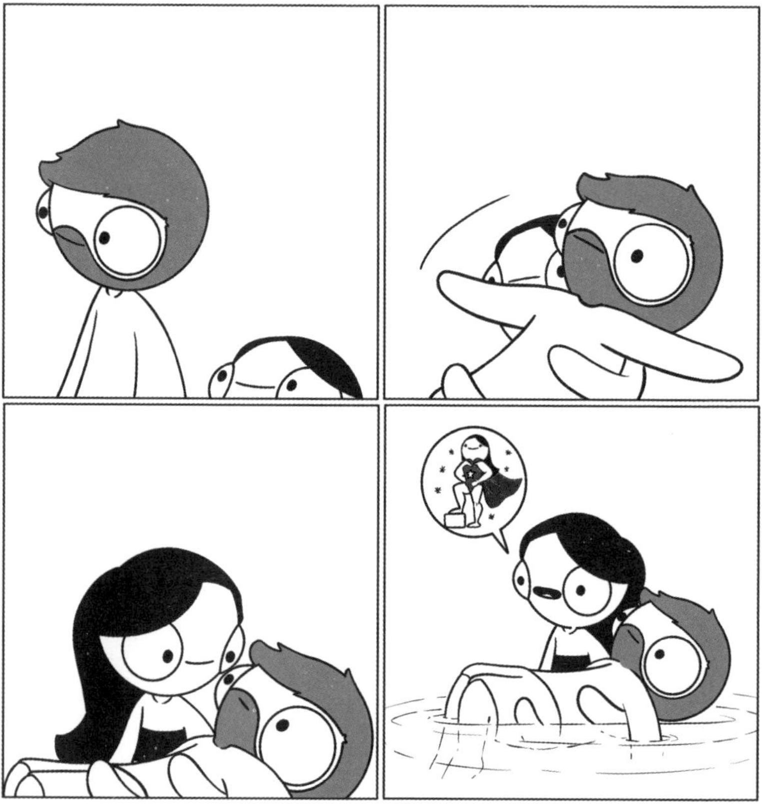

me:

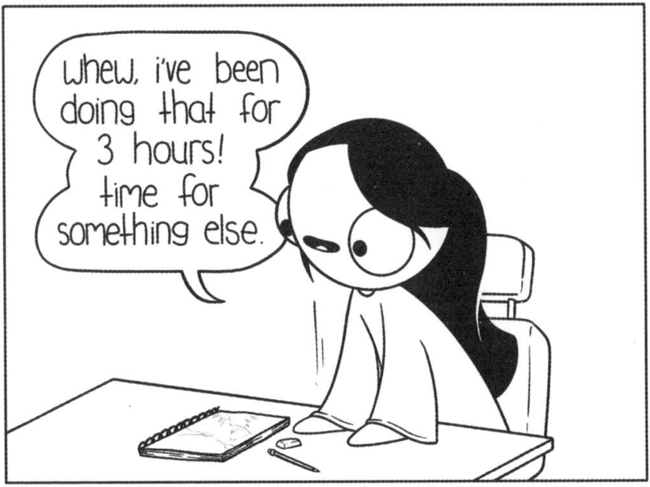
whew, i've been doing that for 3 hours! time for something else.

him:

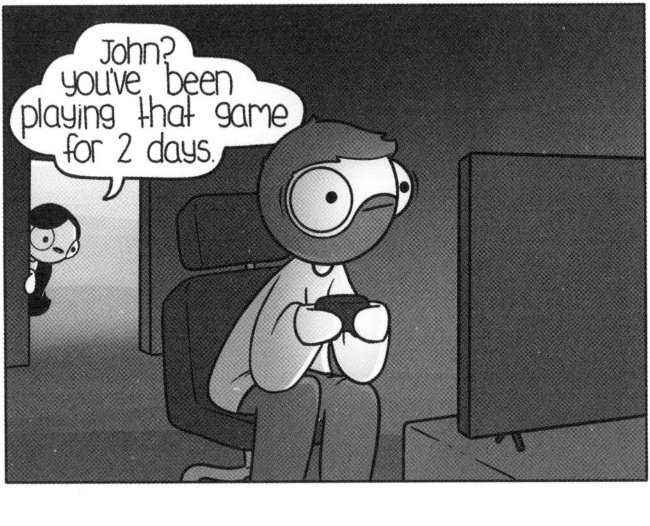
John? you've been playing that game for 2 days.

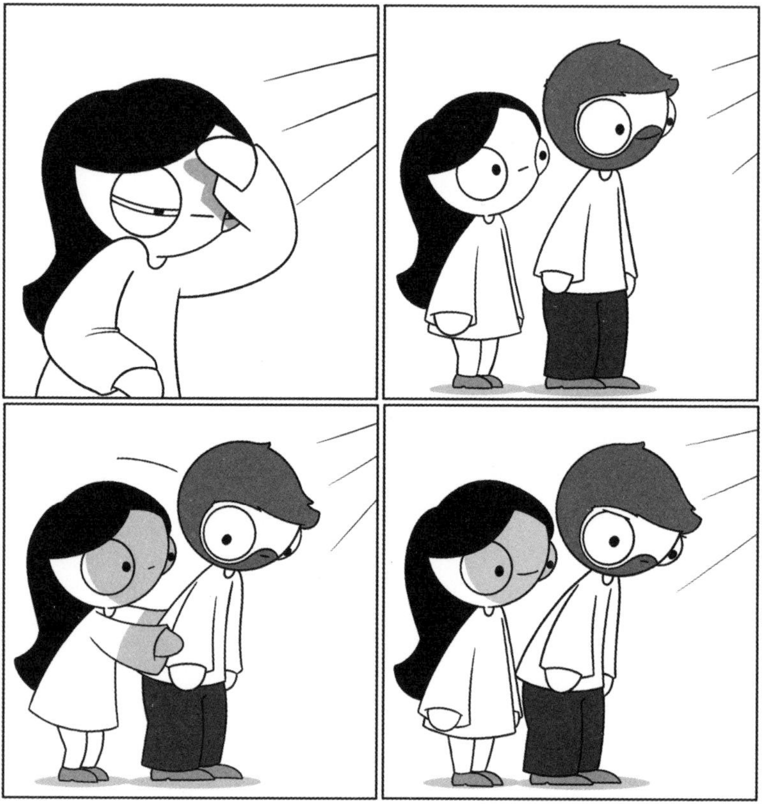

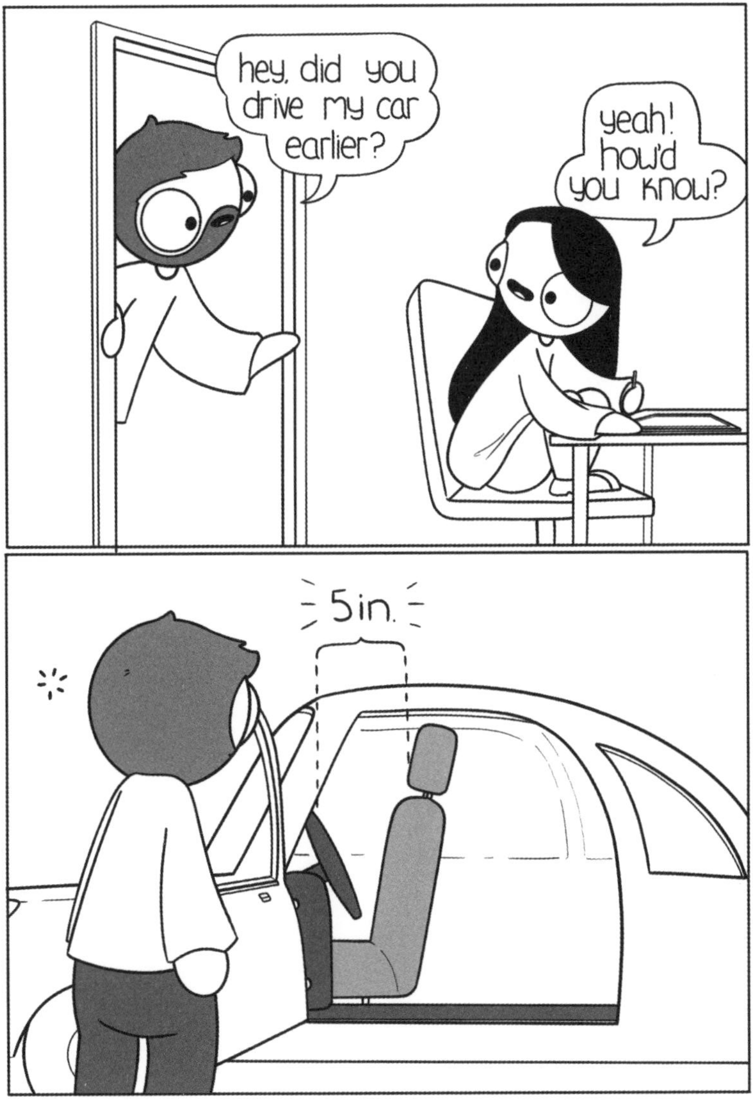
hey, did you drive my car earlier?
yeah! how'd you know?
5in.

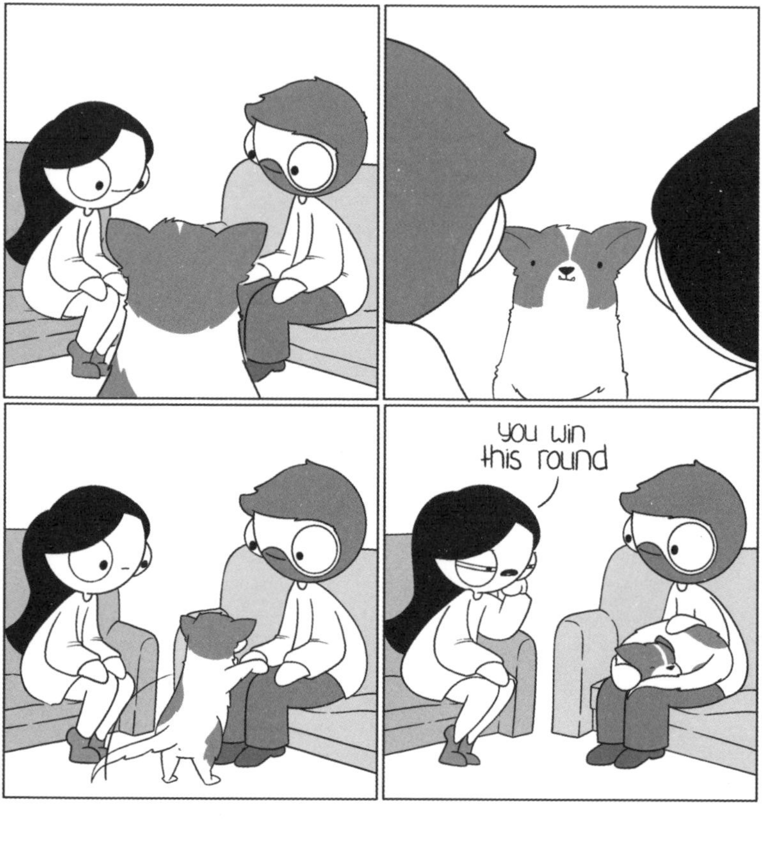
you win
this round

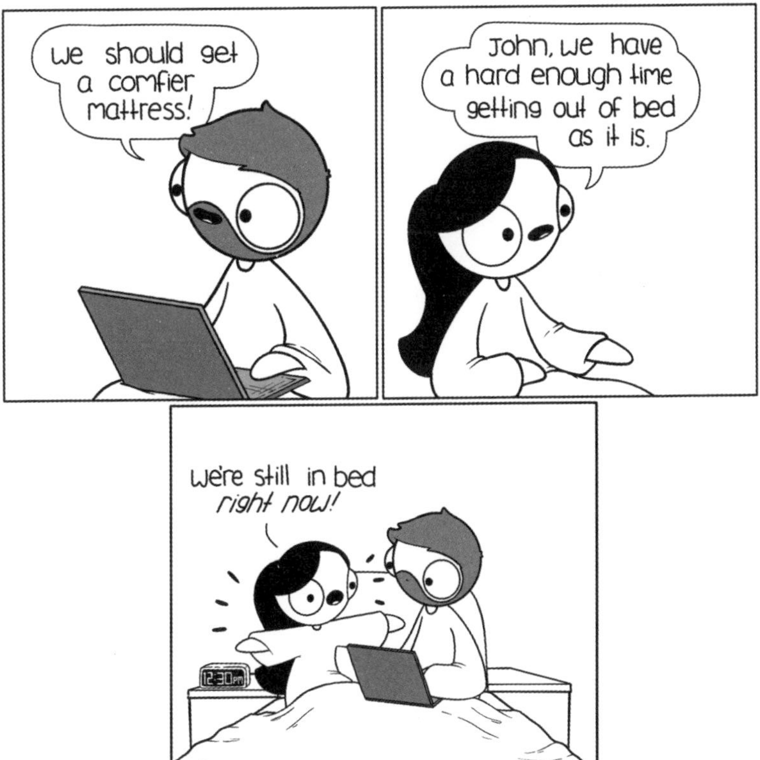
we should get a comfier mattress!
John, we have a hard enough time getting out of bed as it is.
We're still in bed *right now!*
12:30PM

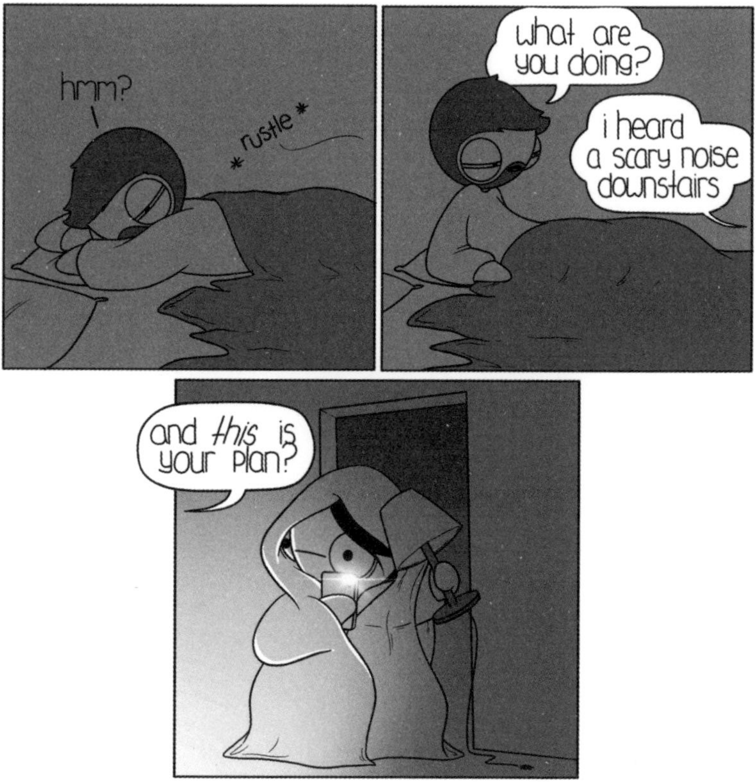
hmm?
*rustle*
what are you doing?
i heard a scary noise downstairs
and *this* is your plan?

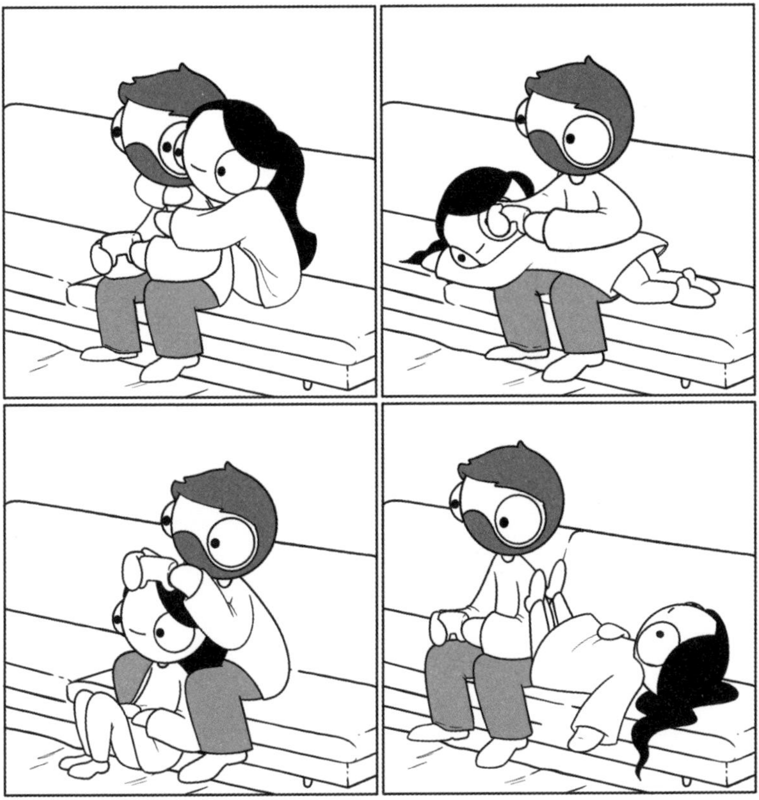

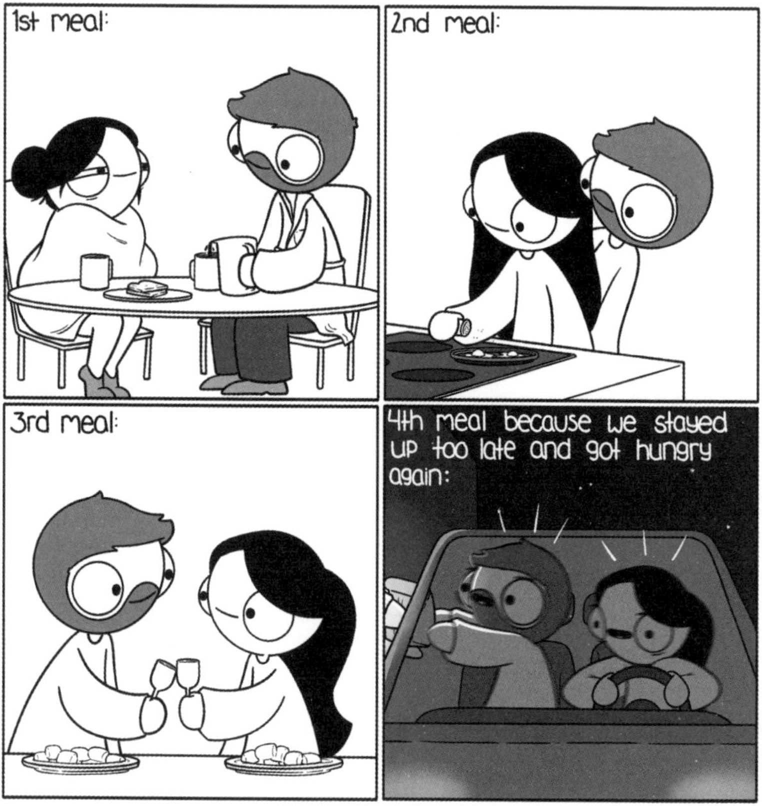
1st meal:
2nd meal:
3rd meal:
4th meal because we stayed up too late and got hungry again:

after a social event:

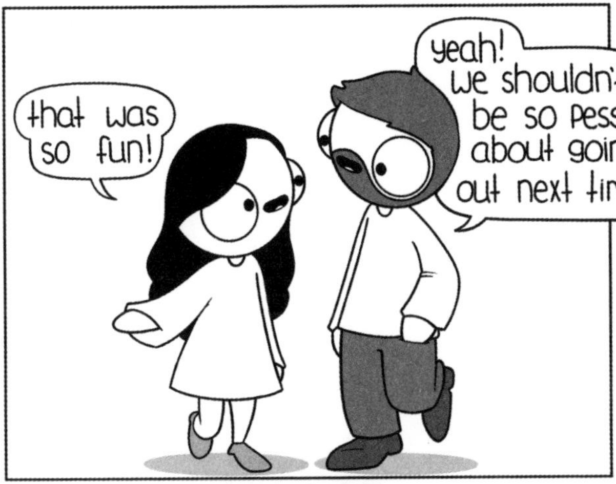
that was so fun!
yeah! we shouldn't be so pessimistic about going out next time.

next time:

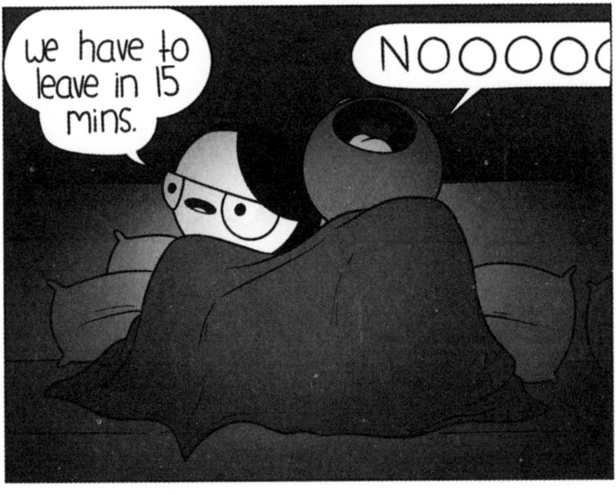
we have to leave in 15 mins.
NOOOO

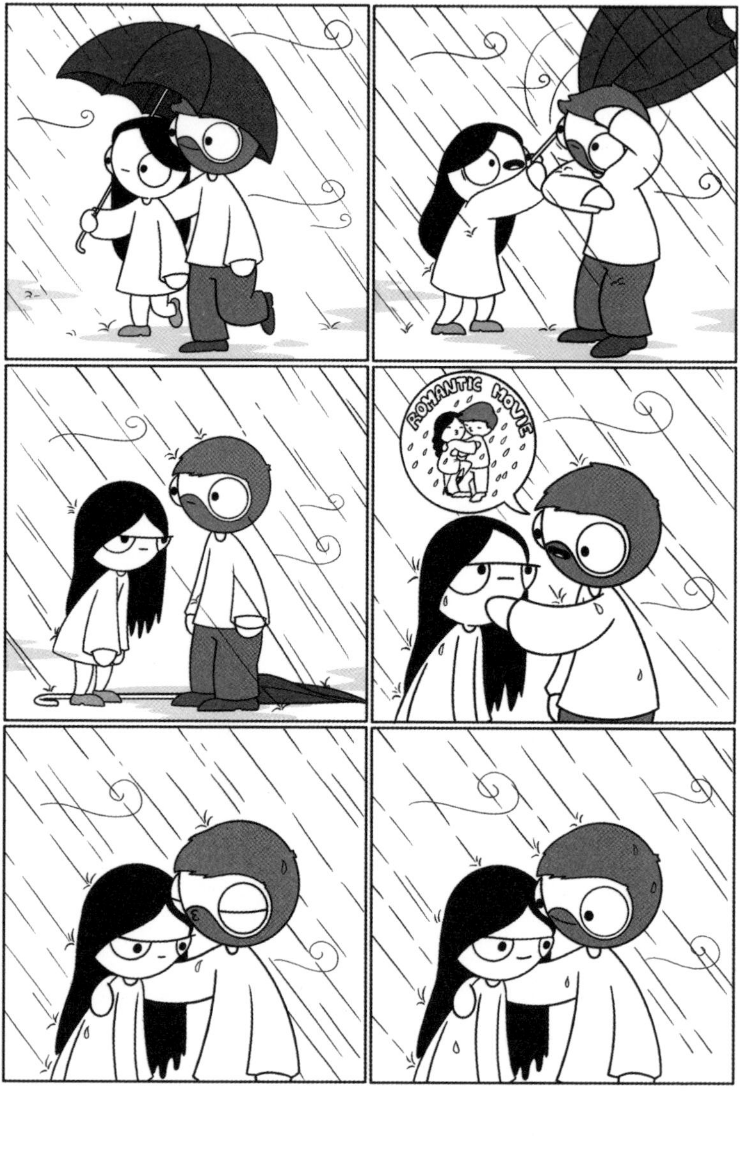
ROMANTIC MOVIE

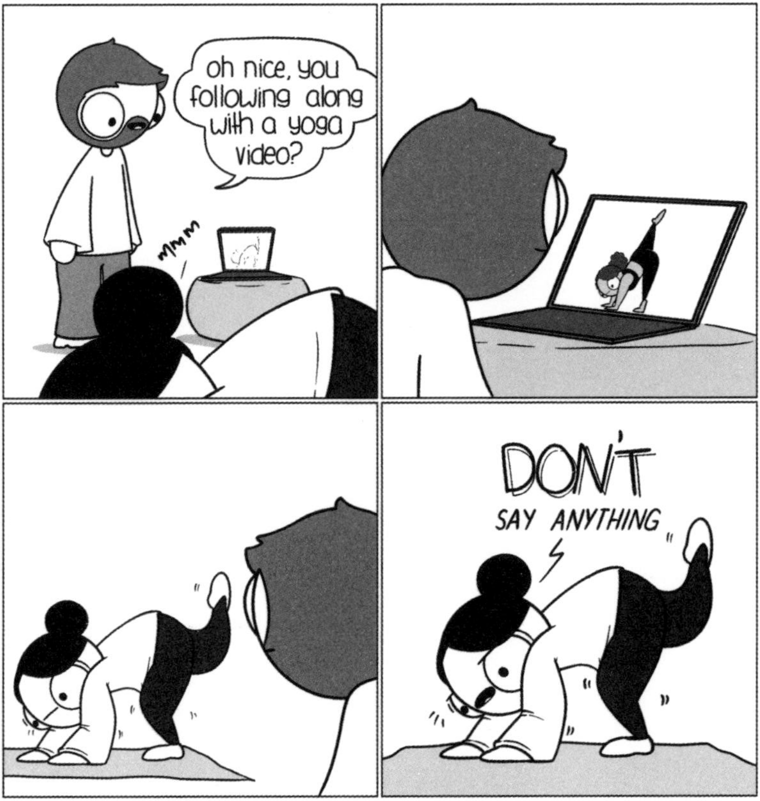
oh nice, you following along with a yoga video?
mmm
DON'T
SAY ANYTHING

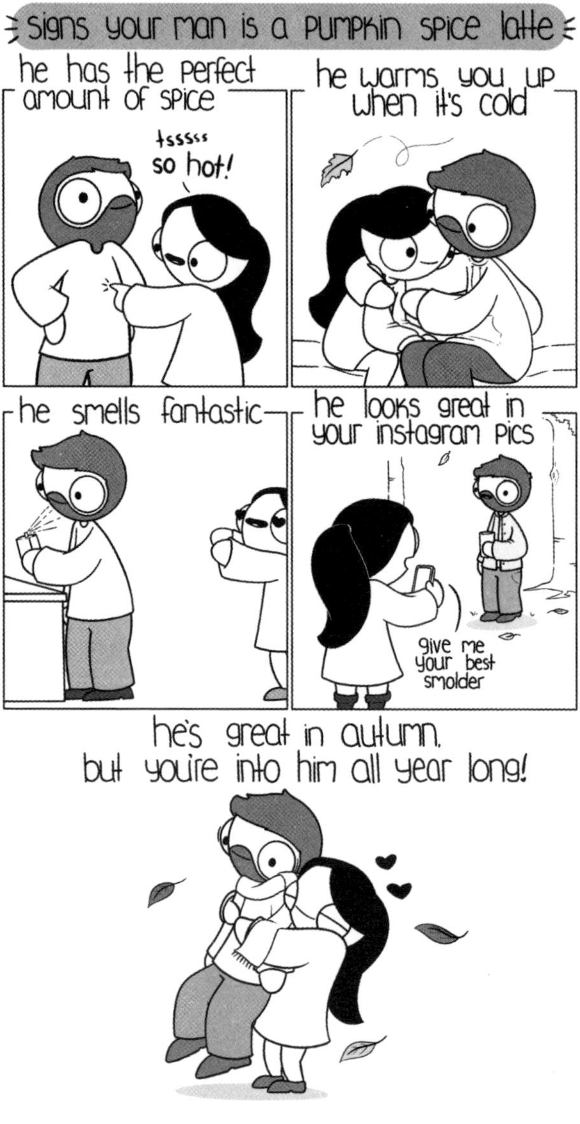
signs your man is a pumpkin spice latte
he has the perfect amount of spice
tssssss
so hot!
he warms you up when it's cold
he smells fantastic
he looks great in your instagram pics
give me your best smolder
he's great in autumn,
but you're into him all year long!

me:

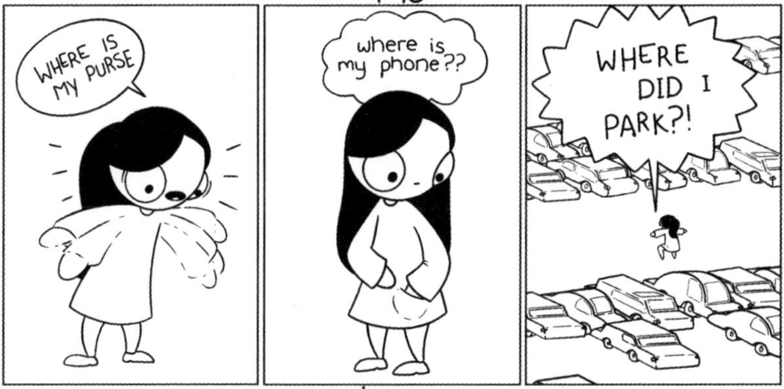
WHERE IS MY PURSE
where is my phone??
WHERE DID I PARK?!

him:

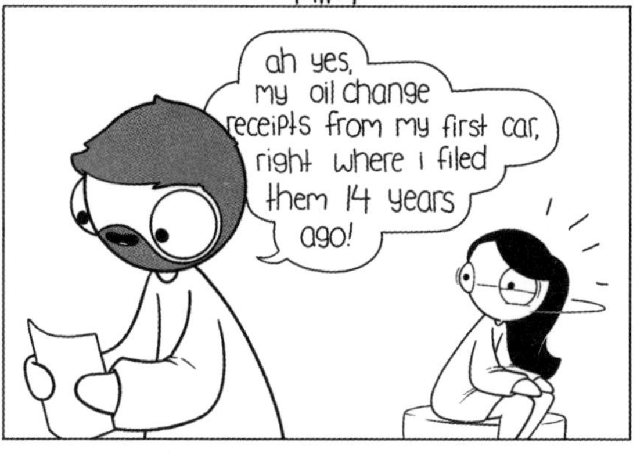
ah yes, my oil change receipts from my first car, right where i filed them 14 years ago!

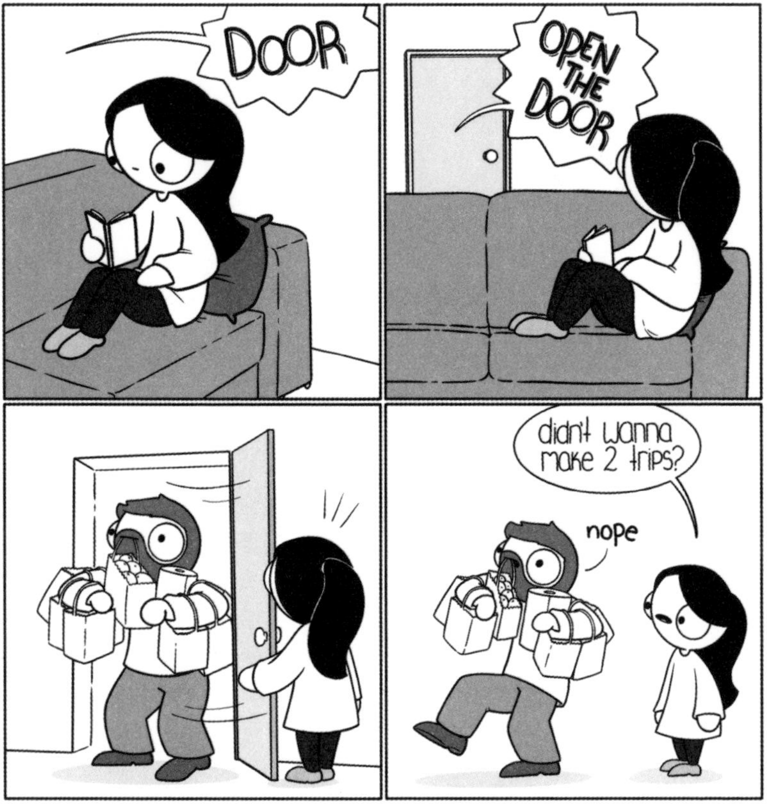
DOOR
OPEN THE DOOR
didn't wanna make 2 trips?
nope

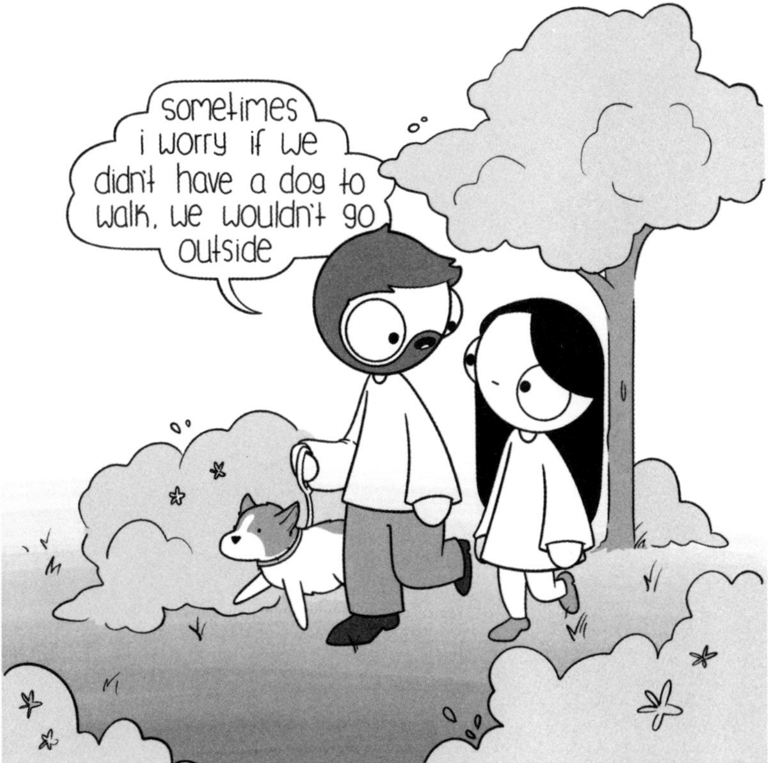
sometimes i worry if we didn't have a dog to walk, we wouldn't go outside

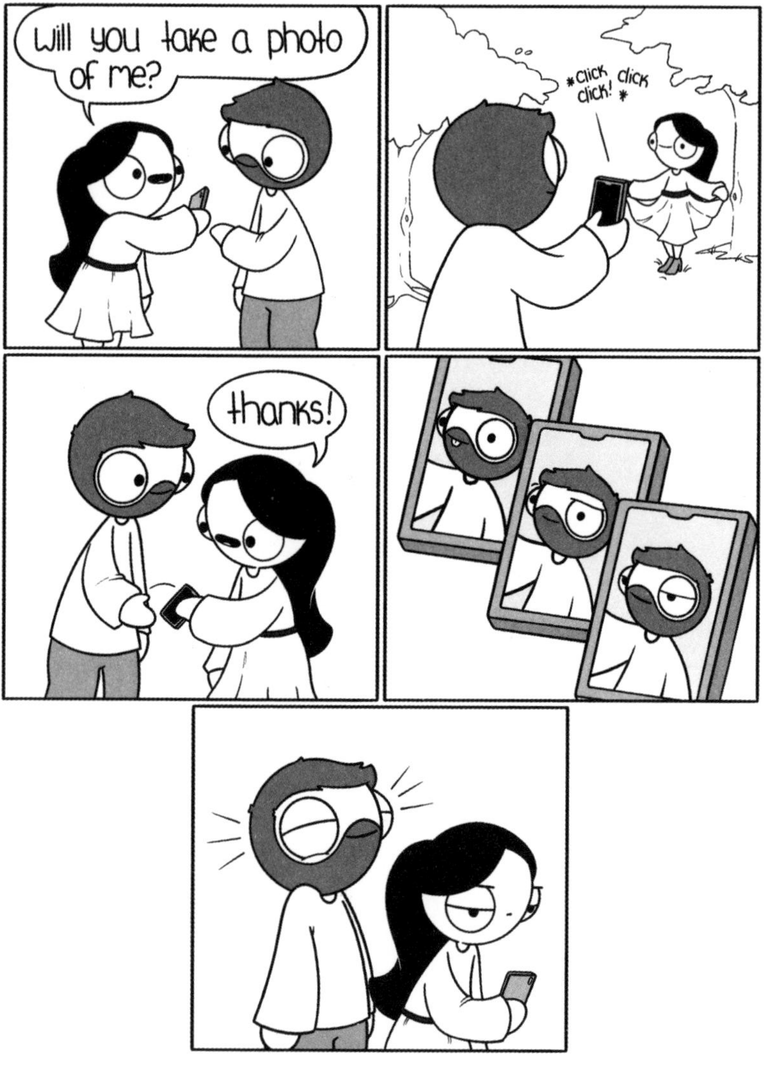
will you take a photo of me?
*click click click!*
thanks!

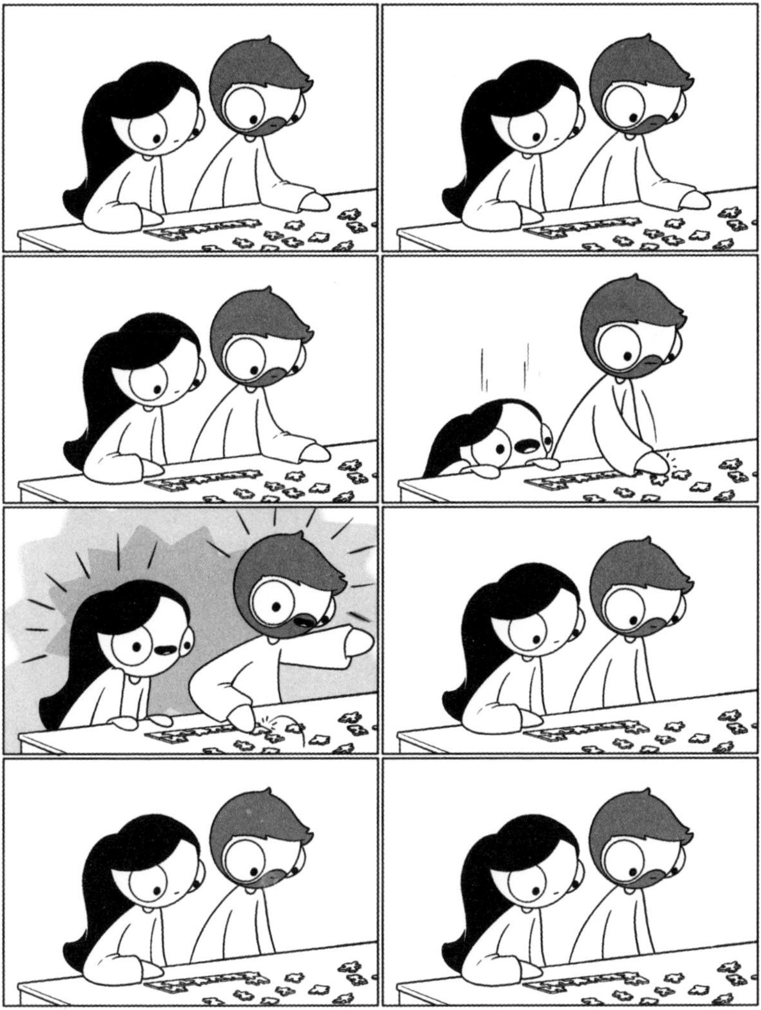

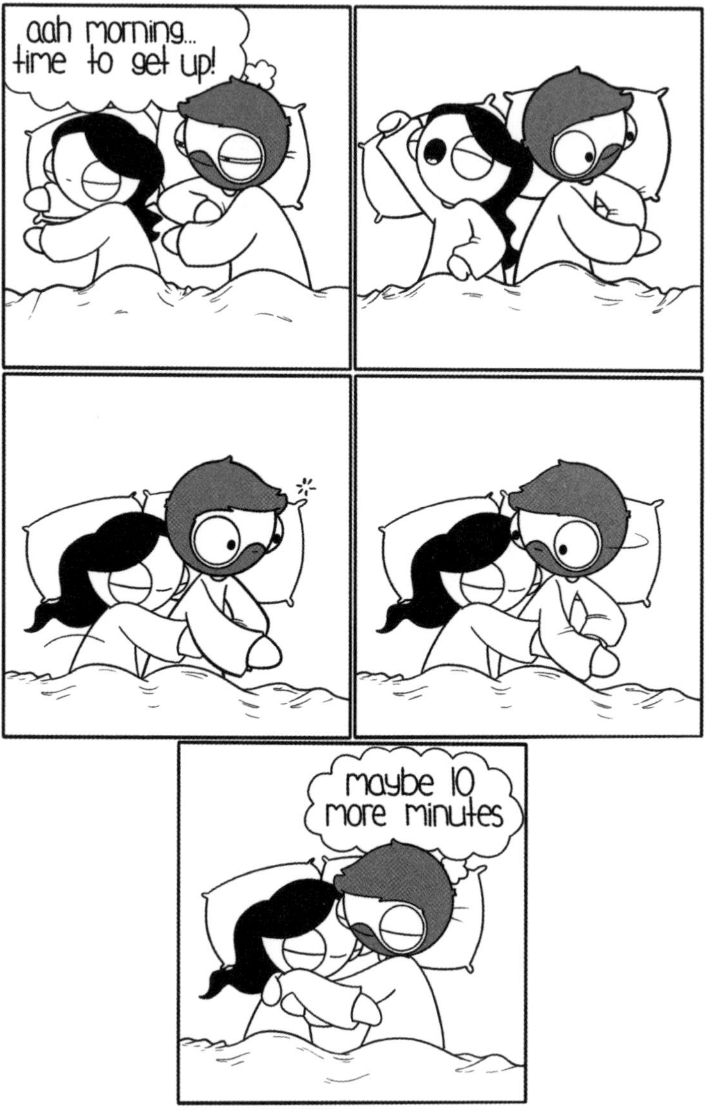
aah morning...
time to get up!
maybe 10
more minutes

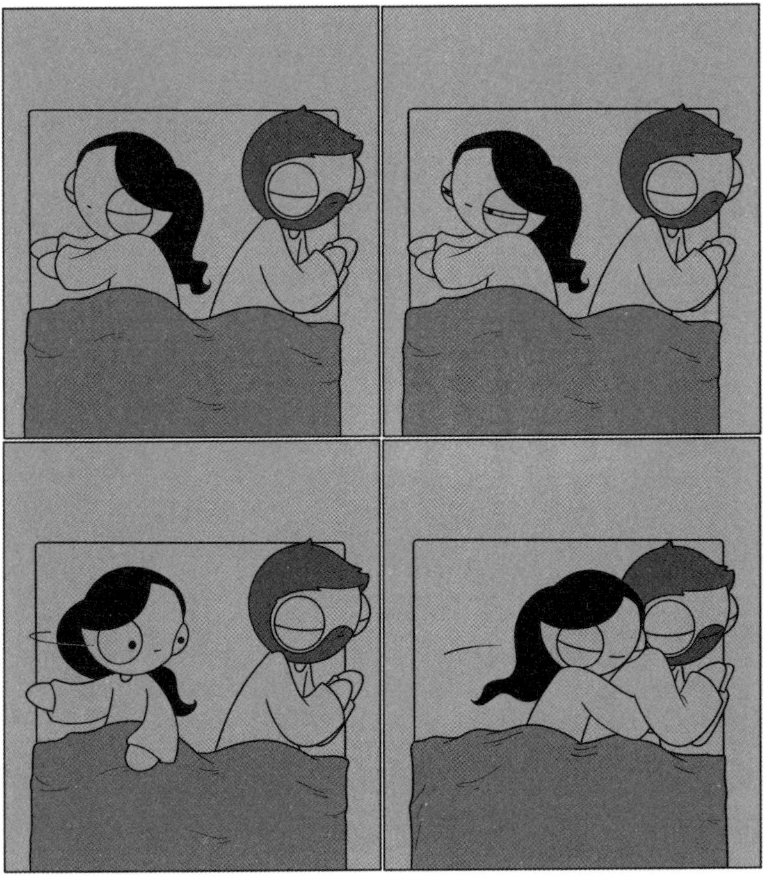

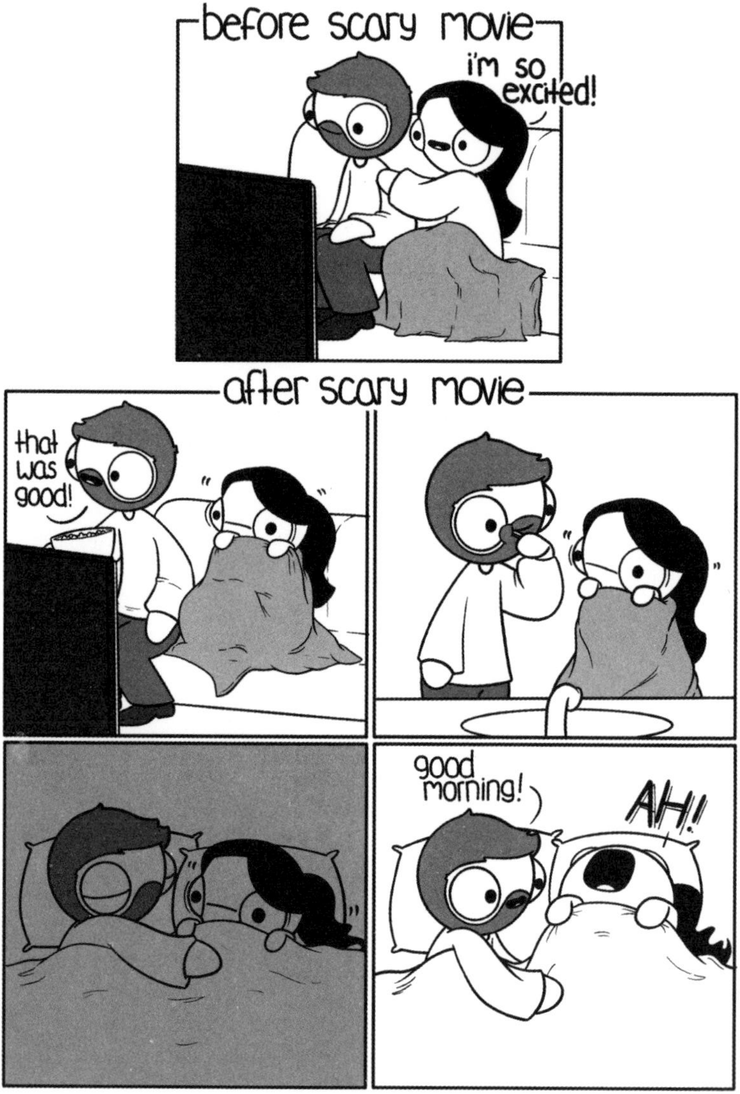

before scary movie
i'm so excited!
after scary movie
that was good!
good morning!
AH!

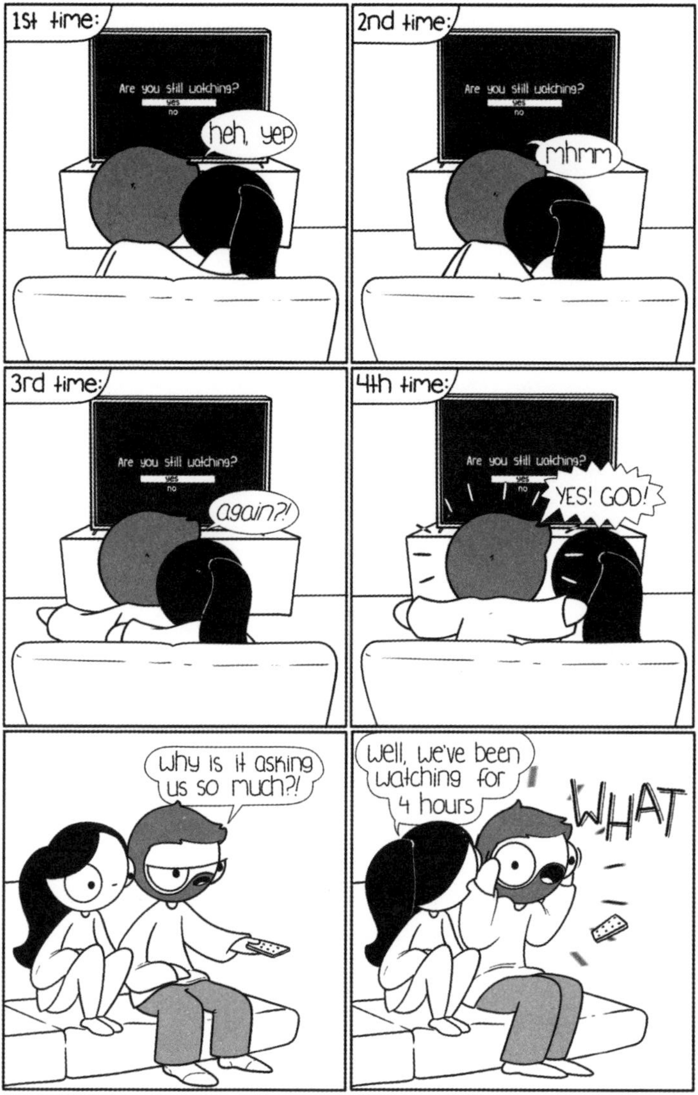

1st time:
Are you still watching?
yes
no
heh, yep
2nd time:
Are you still watching?
yes
no
mhmm
3rd time:
Are you still watching?
yes
no
again?!
4th time:
Are you still watching?
yes
no
YES! GOD!
Why is it asking us so much?!
Well, we've been watching for 4 hours
WHAT

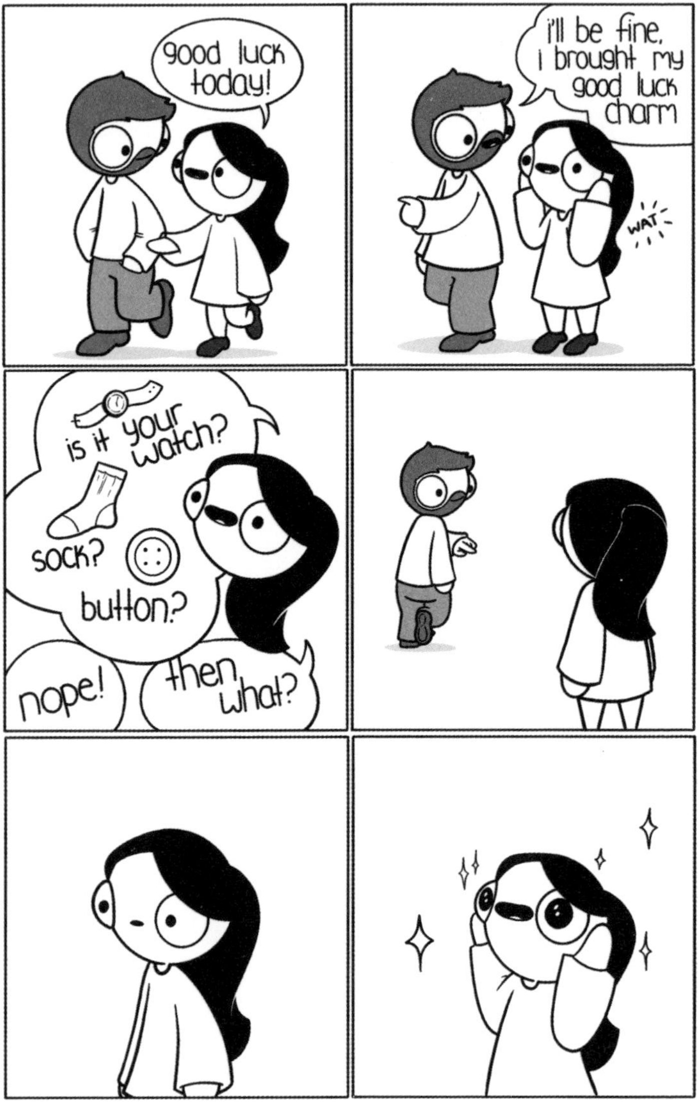
good luck today!
i'll be fine, i brought my good luck charm
WAT
is it your watch?
sock?
button?
nope!
then what?

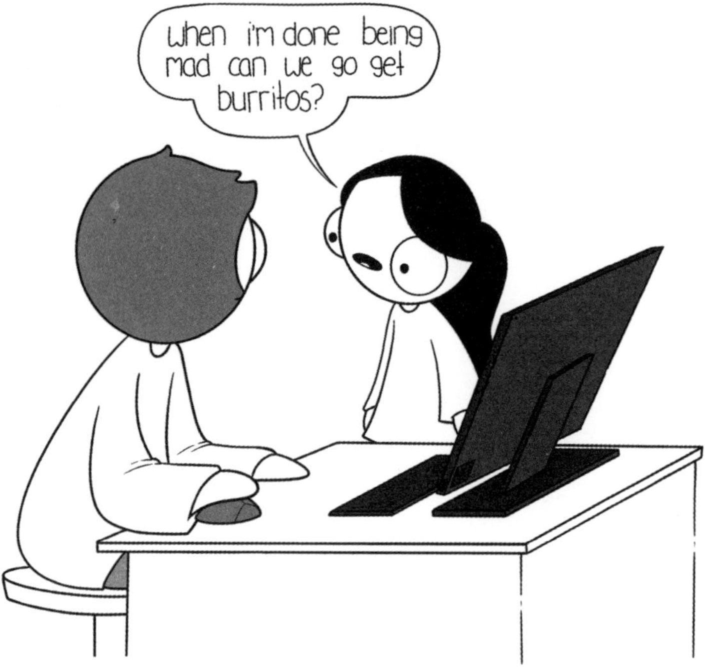
when i'm done being mad can we go get burritos?

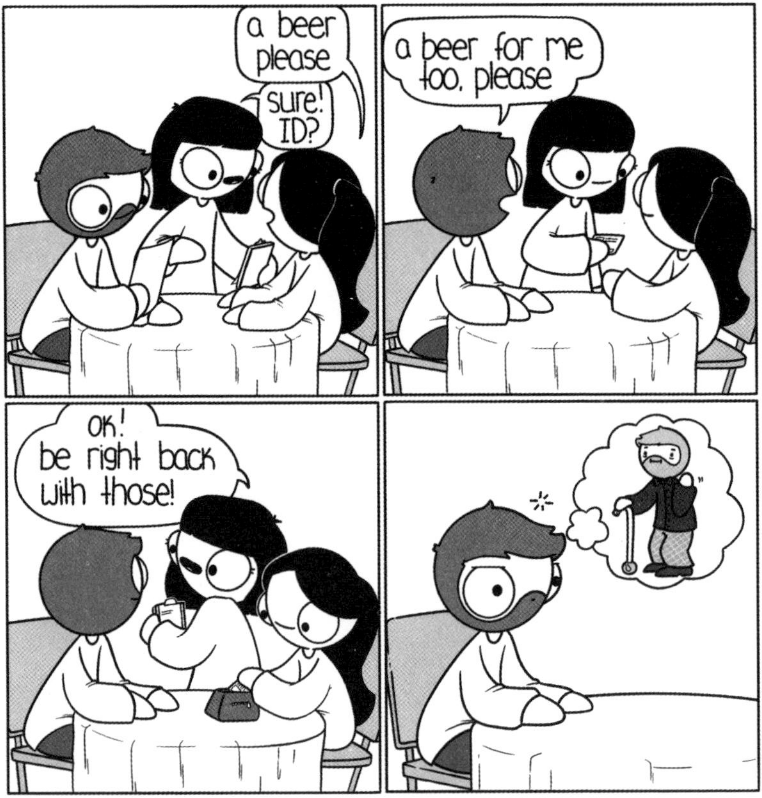
a beer please
sure! ID?
a beer for me too, please
OK! be right back with those!

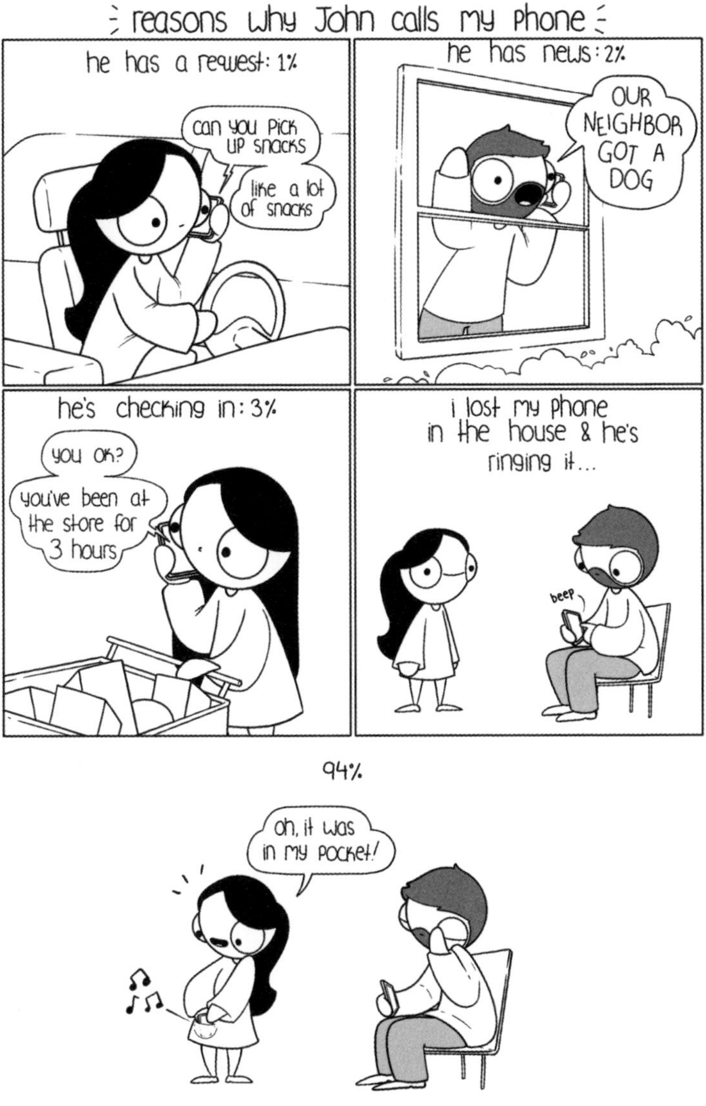
reasons why John calls my phone
he has a request: 1%
can you pick up snacks
like a lot of snacks
he has news: 2%
OUR NEIGHBOR GOT A DOG
he's checking in: 3%
you ok?
you've been at the store for 3 hours
i lost my phone in the house & he's ringing it...
beep
94%
oh, it was in my pocket!

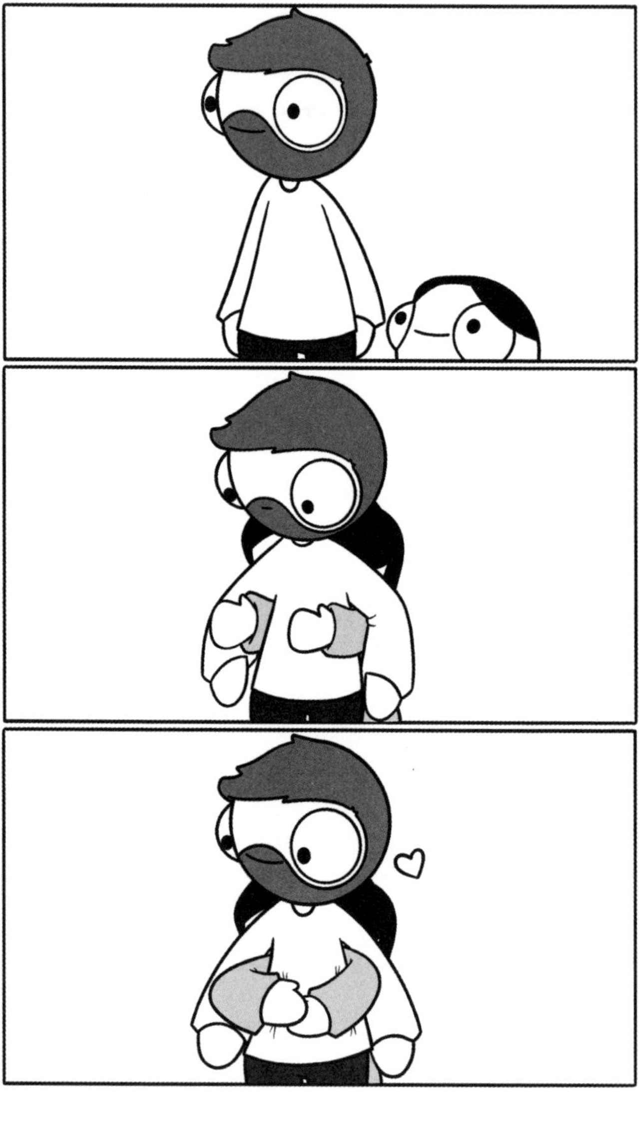

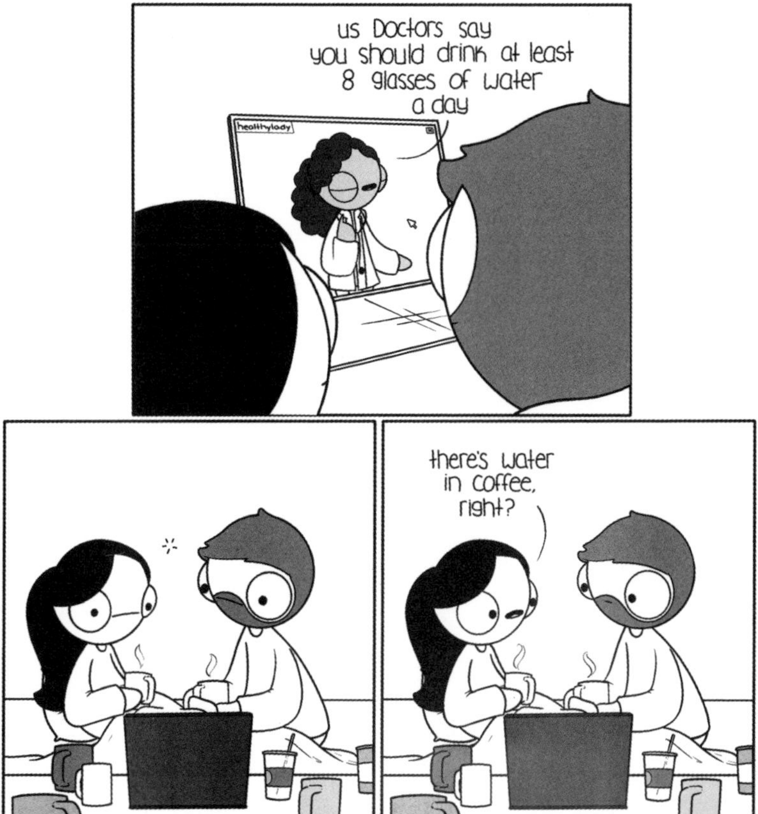
us Doctors say you should drink at least 8 glasses of water a day
healthylady
there's water in coffee, right?

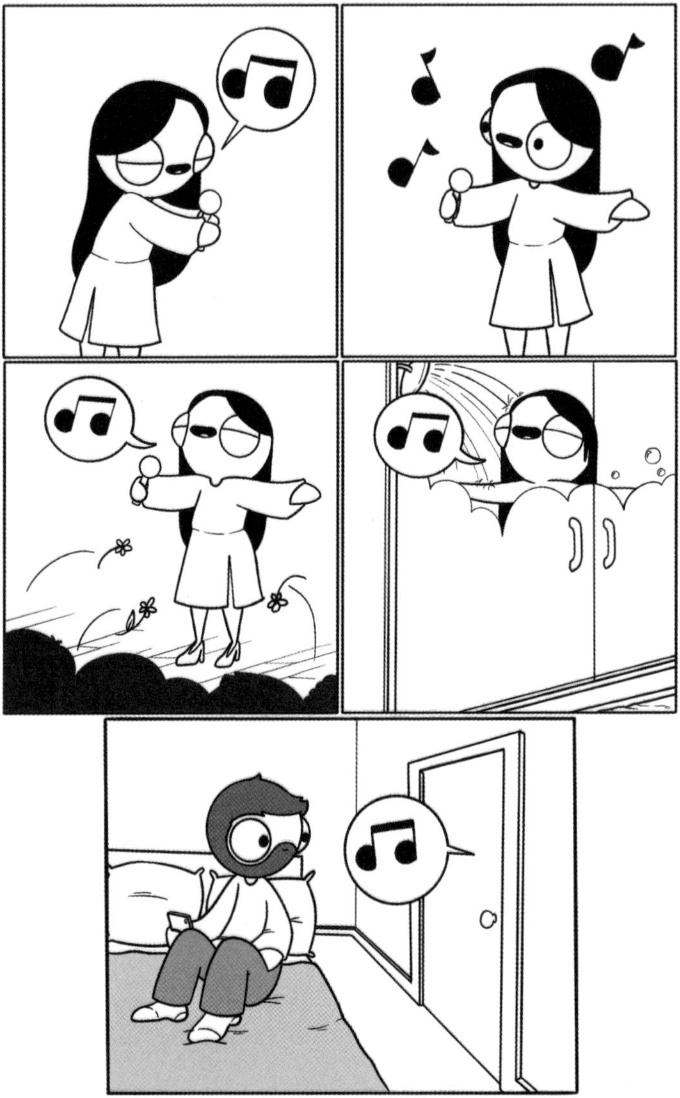

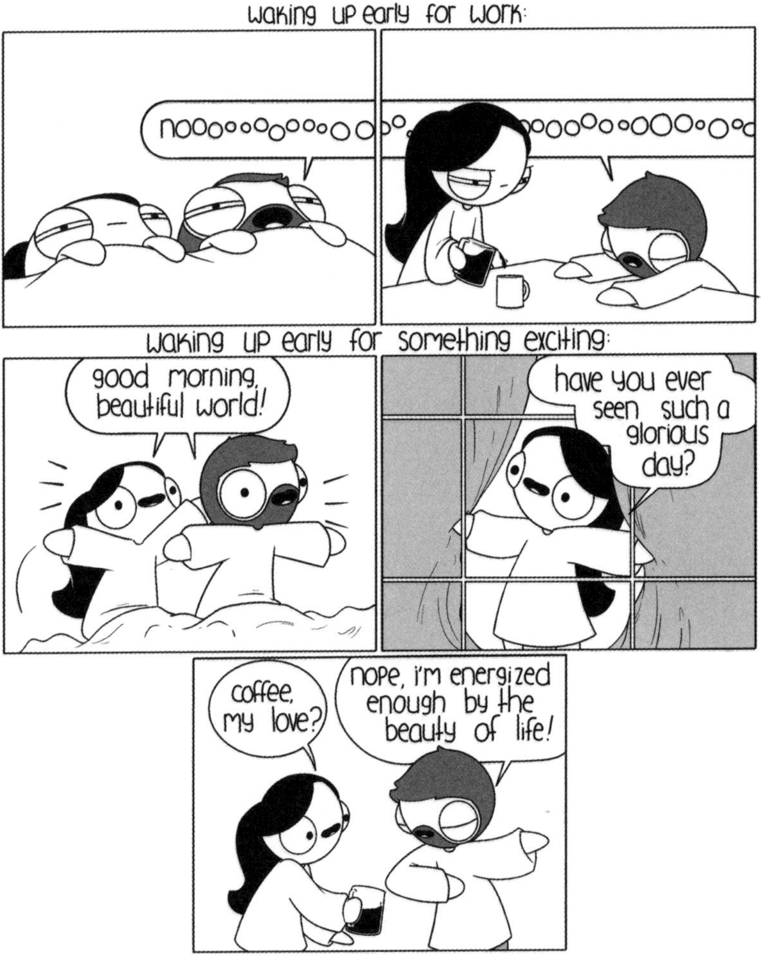
waking up early for work:
nOOoooooooooooooooooooooooooooooo
waking up early for something exciting:
good morning, beautiful world!
have you ever seen such a glorious day?
coffee, my love?
nope, i'm energized enough by the beauty of life!

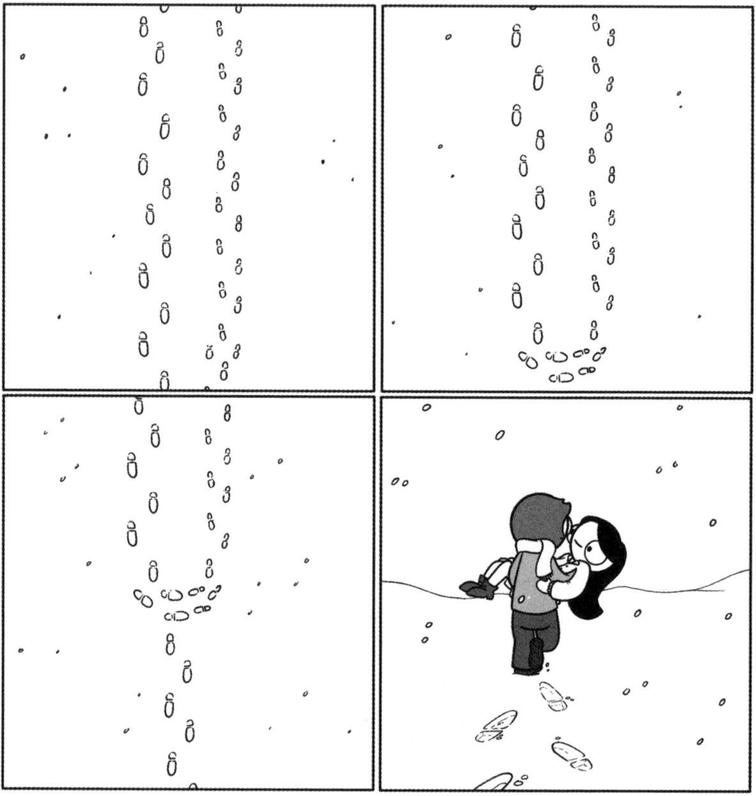

# reasons why we clean

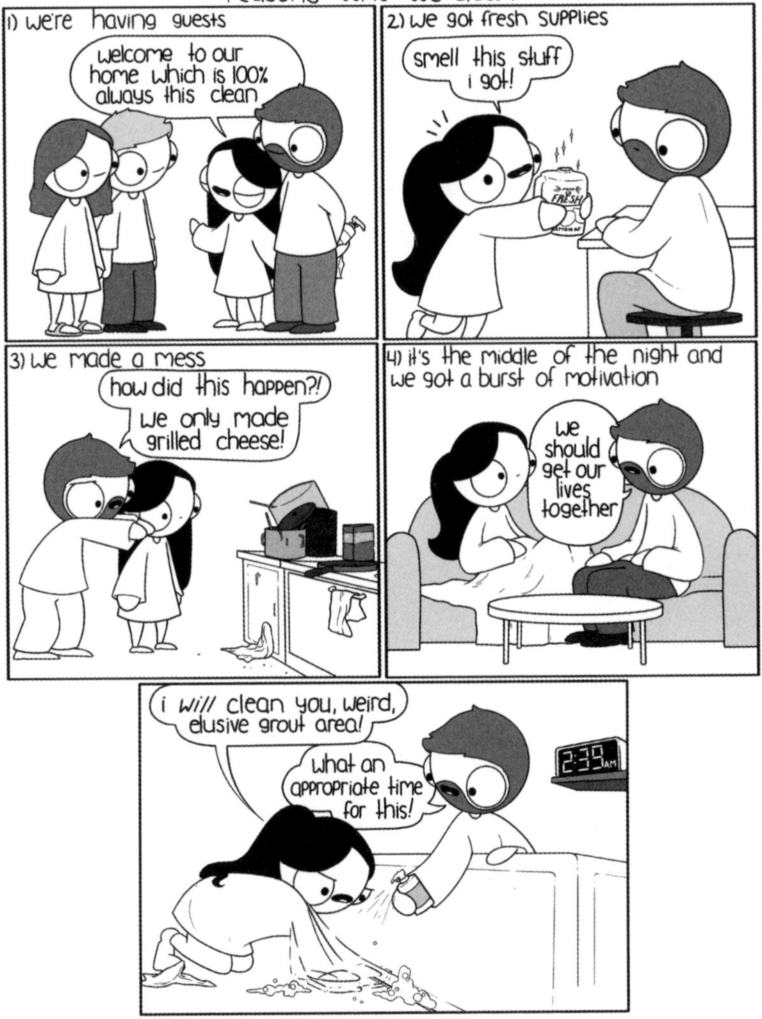
1) we're having guests
welcome to our home which is 100% always this clean
2) we got fresh supplies
smell this stuff i got!
FRESH
3) we made a mess
how did this happen?!
we only made grilled cheese!
4) it's the middle of the night and we got a burst of motivation
we should get our lives together
i *will* clean you, weird, elusive grout area!
what an appropriate time for this!
2:39 AM

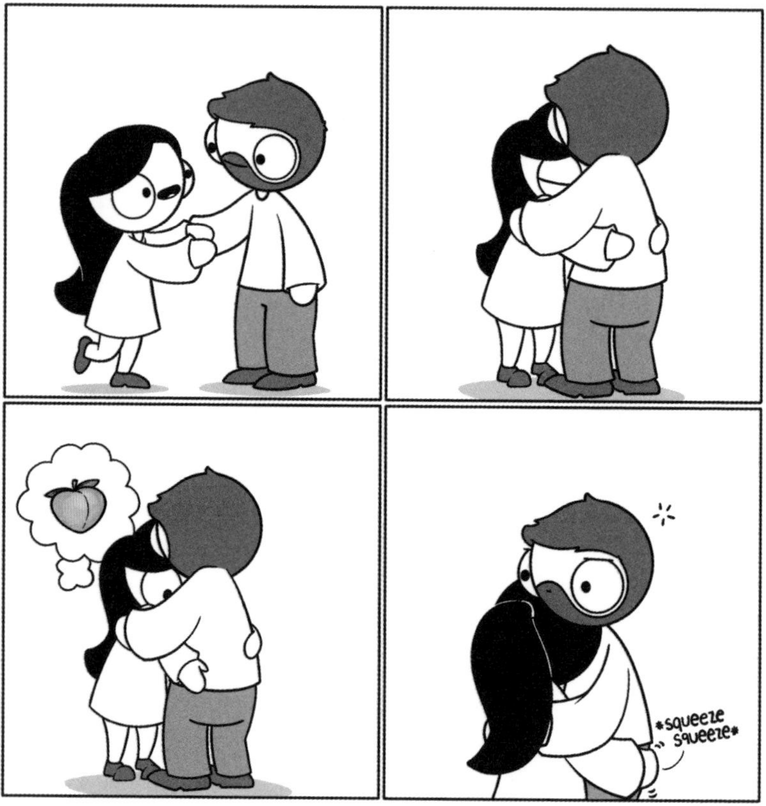
*squeeze
squeeze*

us: definitely not in the market for a house
also us:

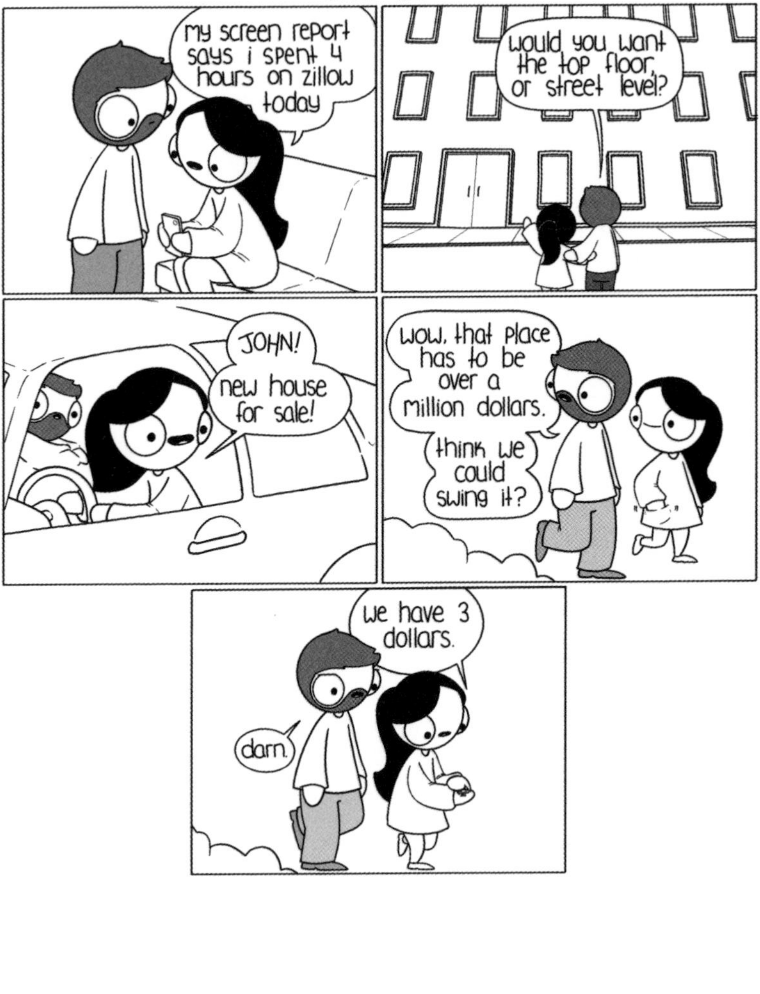
my screen report says i spent 4 hours on zillow today
would you want the top floor, or street level?
JOHN!
new house for sale!
wow, that place has to be over a million dollars.
think we could swing it?
we have 3 dollars.
darn.

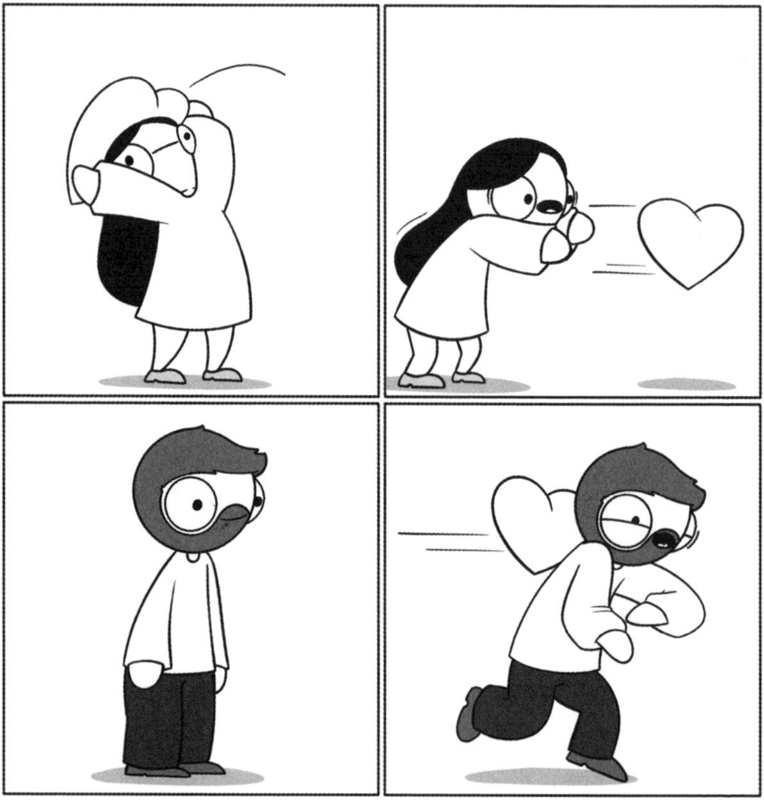

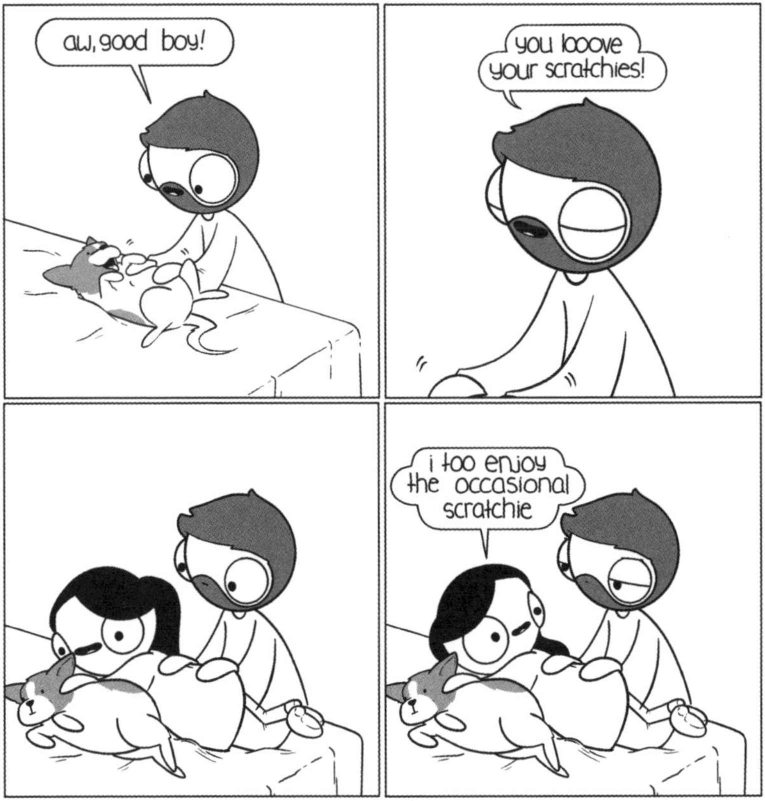
aw, good boy!
you looove your scratchies!
i too enjoy the occasional scratchie

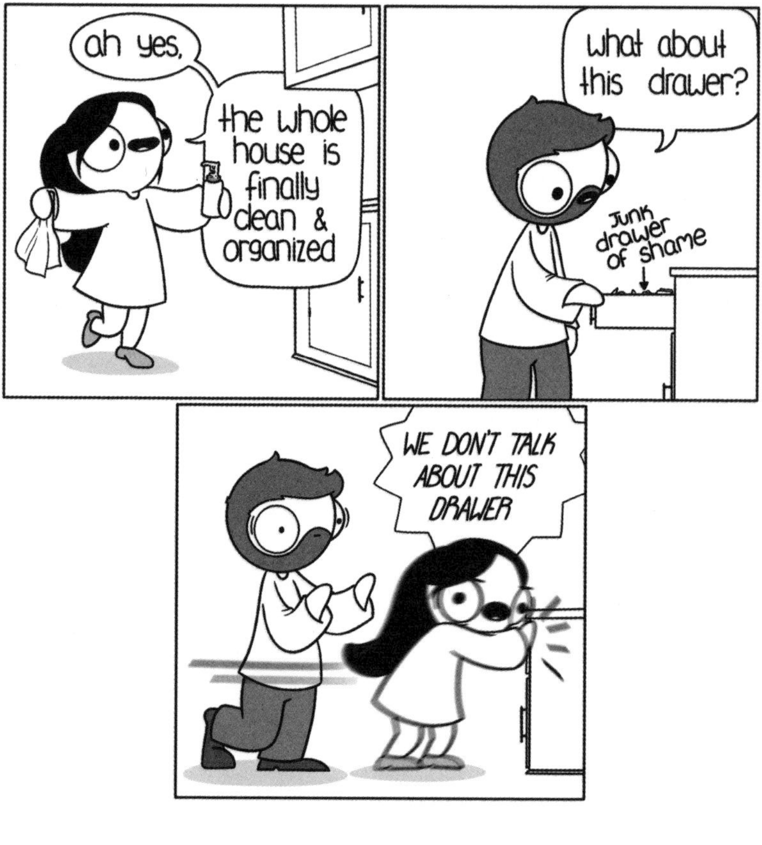
ah yes,
the whole house is finally clean & organized
what about this drawer?
Junk drawer of shame
WE DON'T TALK ABOUT THIS DRAWER

what i should wear out to the car:

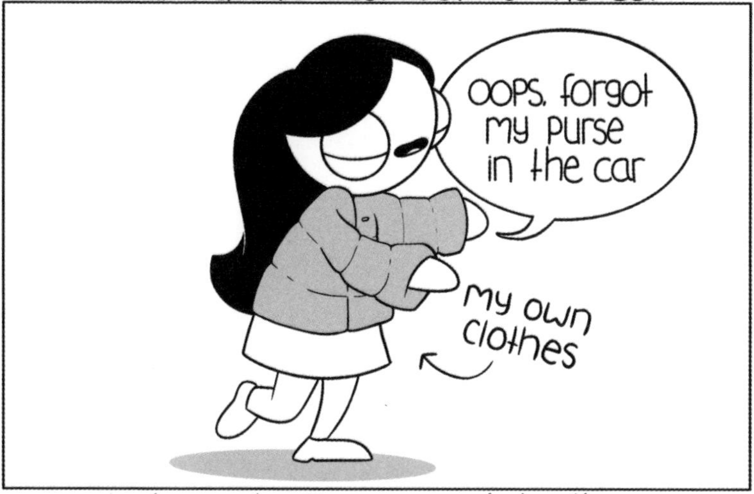
OOPS. forgot my purse in the car
my own clothes

what i actually wear out to the car:

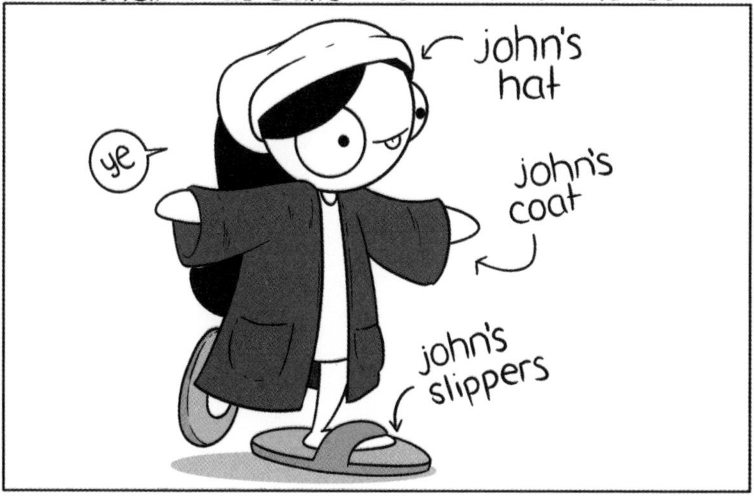
john's hat
ye
john's coat
john's slippers

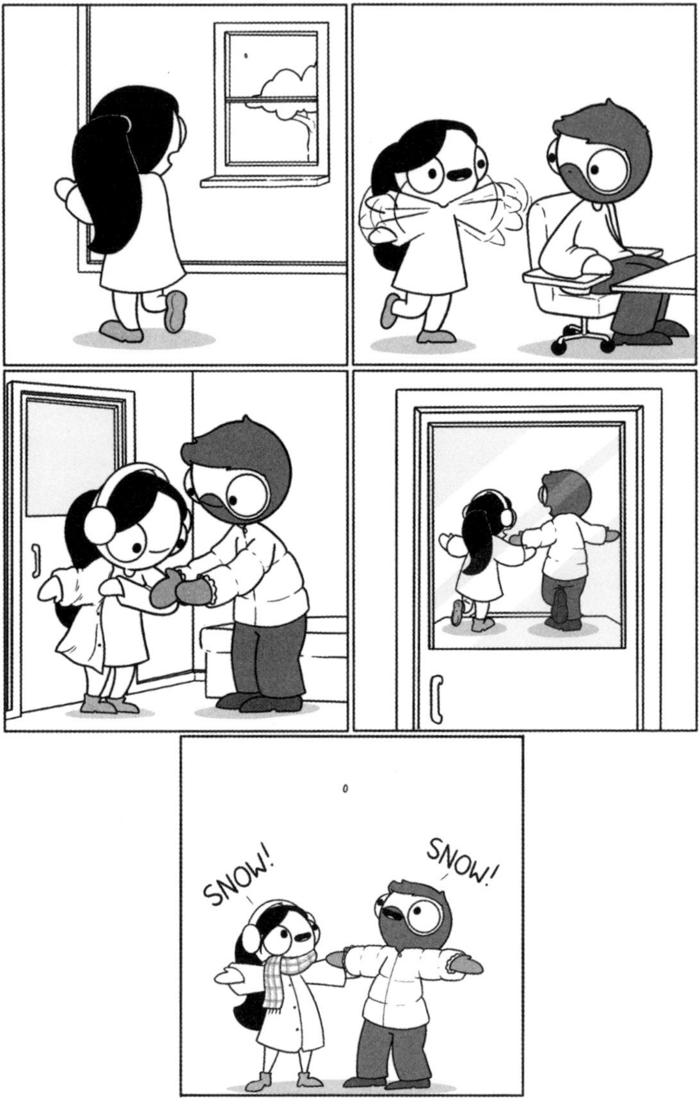
SNOW!
SNOW!

summer:
flowy dresses
clean & fresh
trendy shoes
winter:
what are you wearing under your blanket?
another blanket

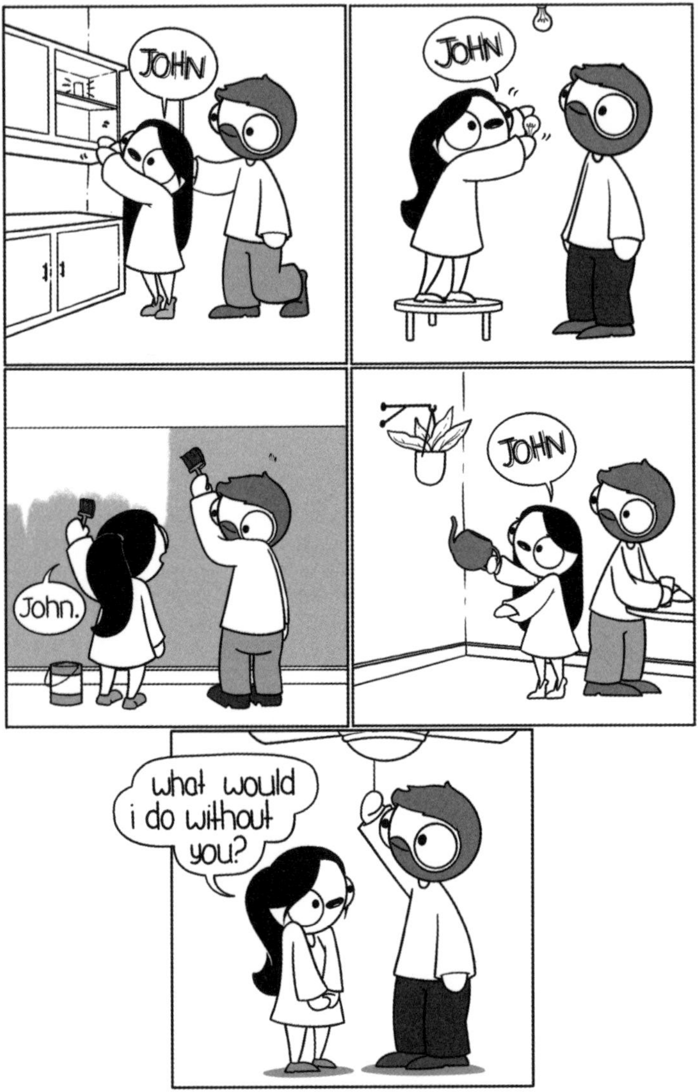
JOHN
JOHN
John.
JOHN
what would i do without you?

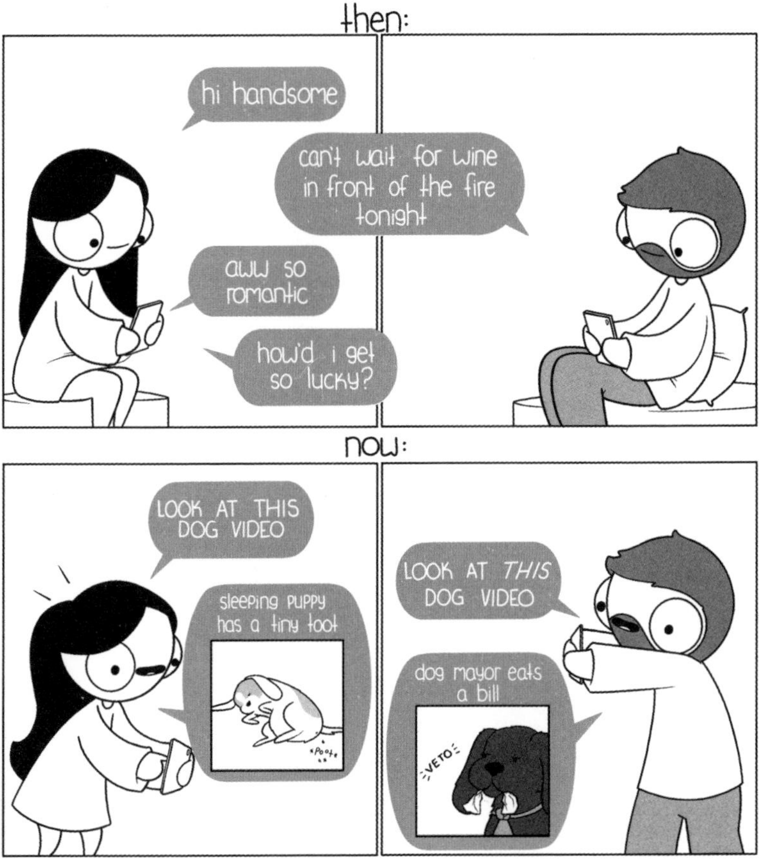
then:
hi handsome
can't wait for wine in front of the fire tonight
aww so romantic
how'd i get so lucky?
now:
LOOK AT THIS DOG VIDEO
sleeping puppy has a tiny toot
LOOK AT *THIS* DOG VIDEO
dog mayor eats a bill
VETO

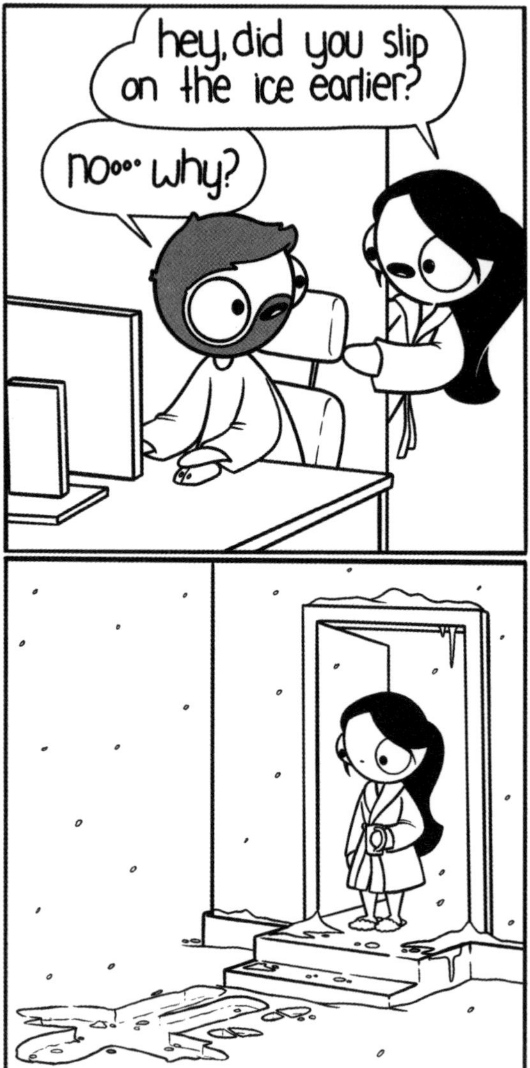
hey, did you slip on the ice earlier?
no... why?

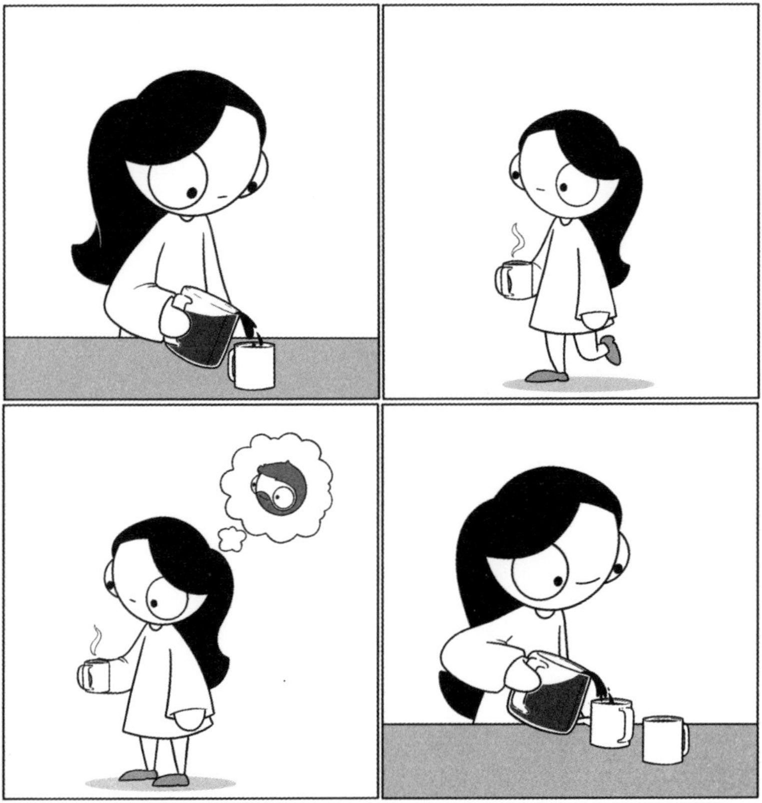

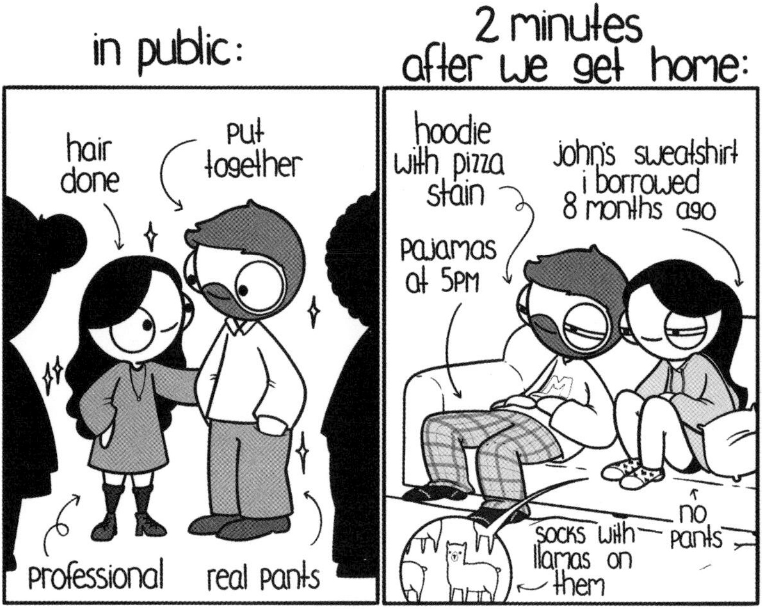
in public:
hair done
put together
professional
real pants
2 minutes after we get home:
hoodie with pizza stain
john's sweatshirt i borrowed 8 months ago
pajamas at 5PM
socks with llamas on them
no pants

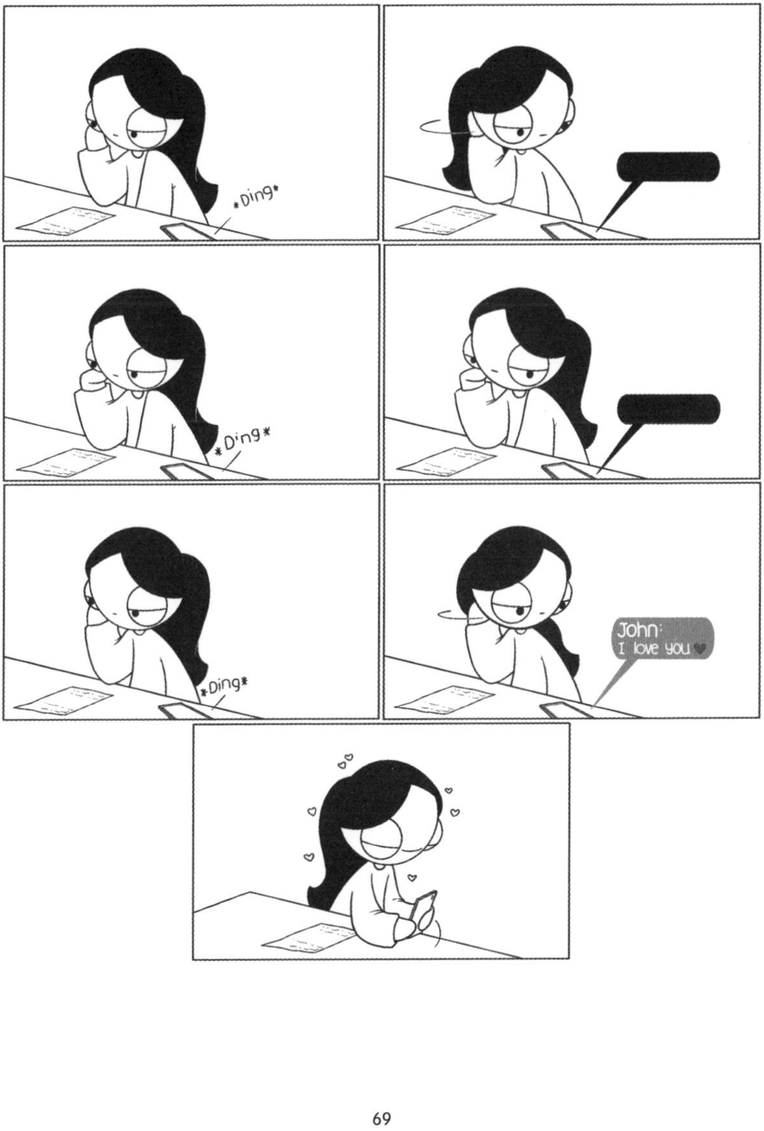
*Ding*
*Ding*
*Ding*
John:
I love you

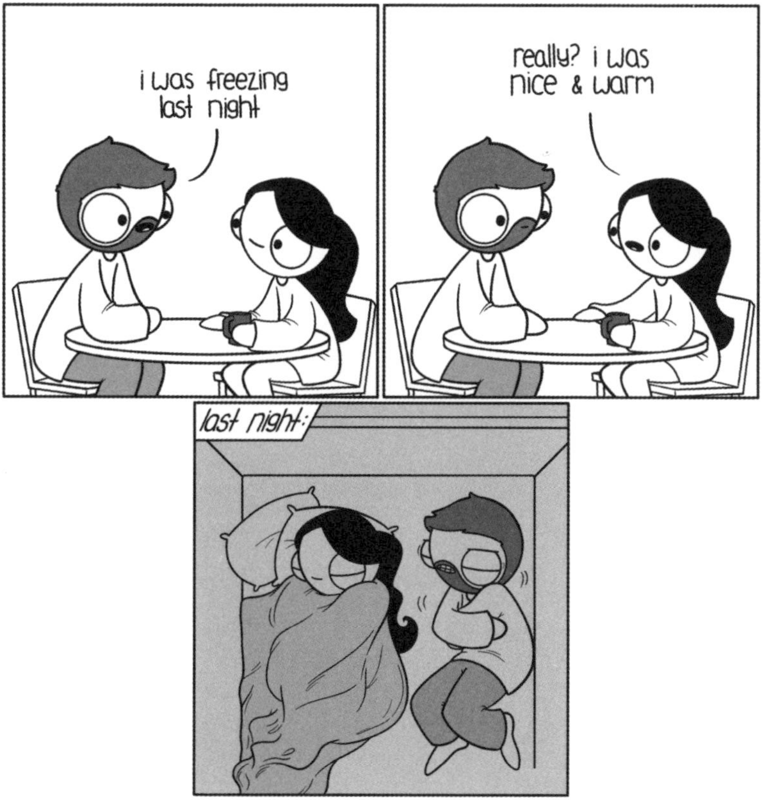
i was freezing last night
really? i was nice & warm
last night:

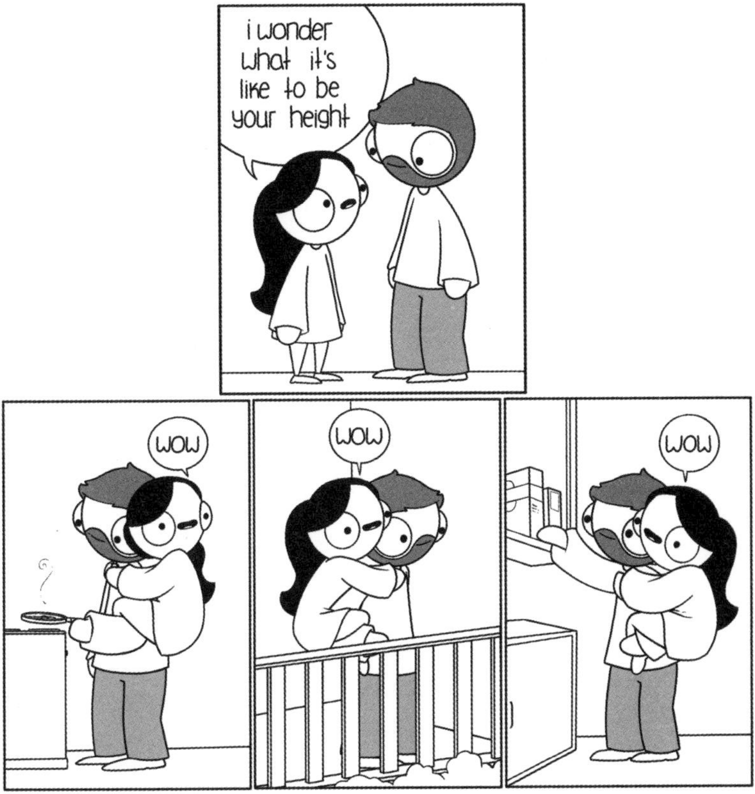
i wonder what it's like to be your height
WOW
WOW
WOW

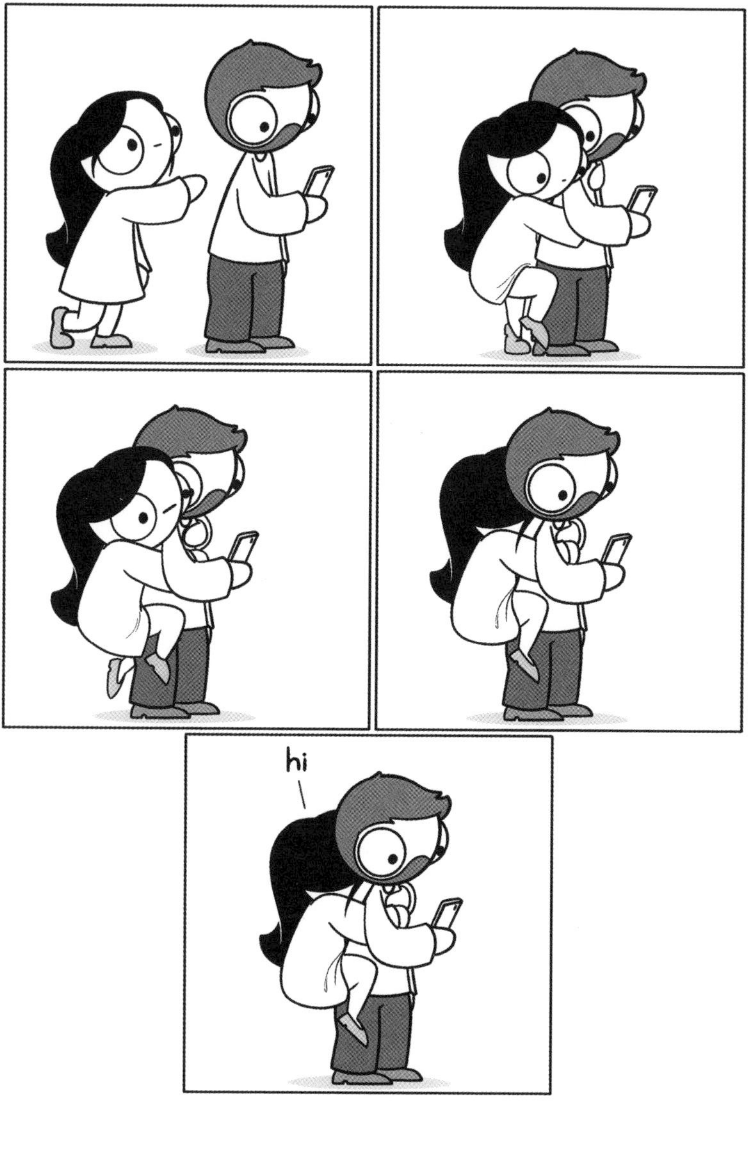
hi

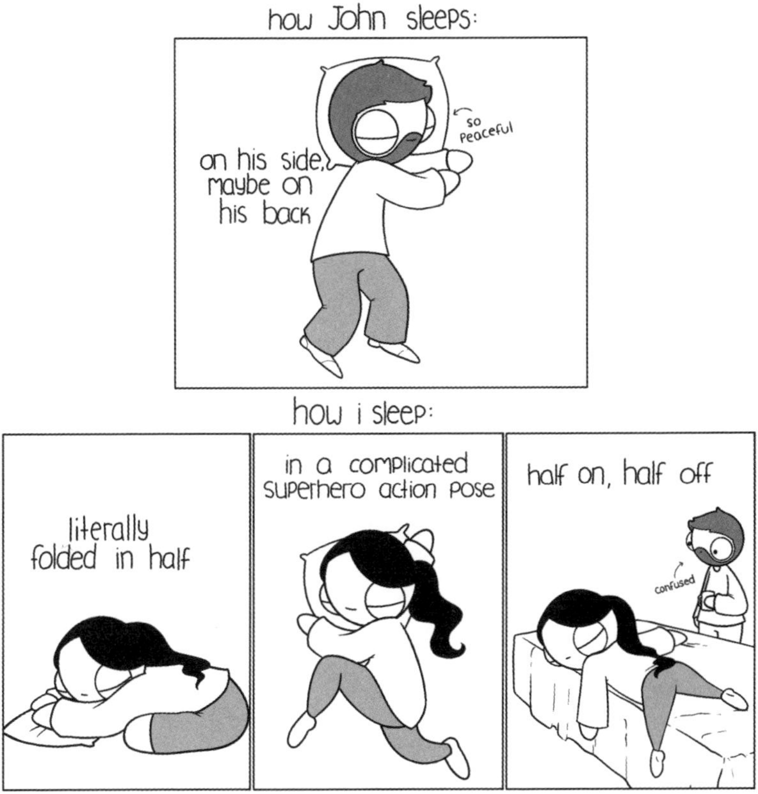
how John sleeps:
on his side, maybe on his back
so peaceful
how i sleep:
literally folded in half
in a complicated superhero action pose
half on, half off
confused

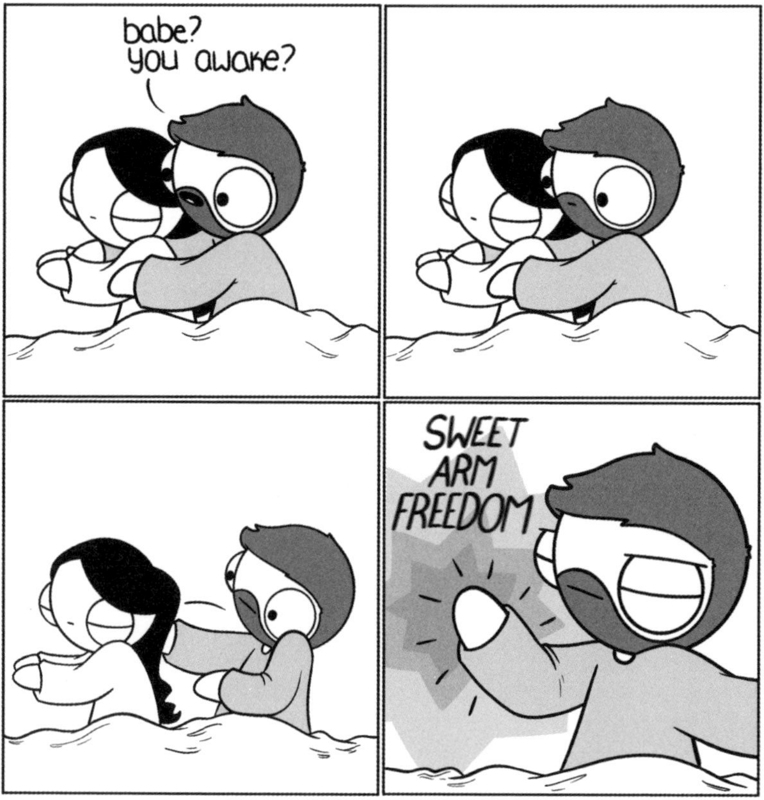
babe?
you awake?
SWEET
ARM
FREEDOM

# things we have no self-control with

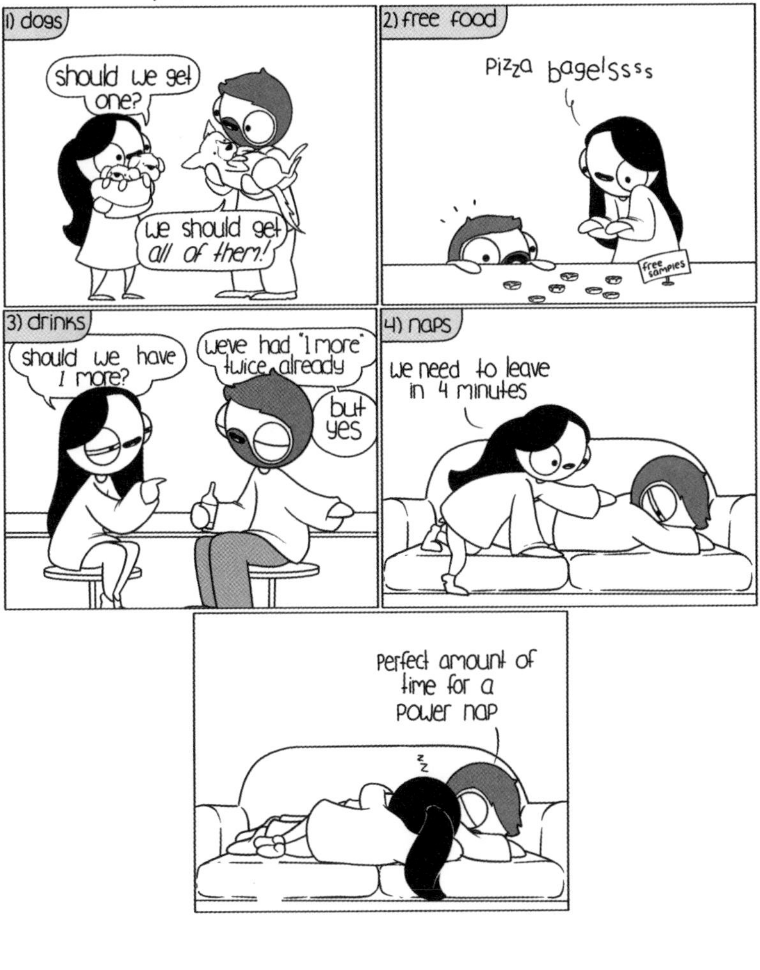
1) dogs
should we get one?
we should get all of them!
2) free food
Pizza bagelssss
free samples
3) drinks
should we have 1 more?
we've had "1 more" twice already
but yes
4) naps
we need to leave in 4 minutes
perfect amount of time for a power nap

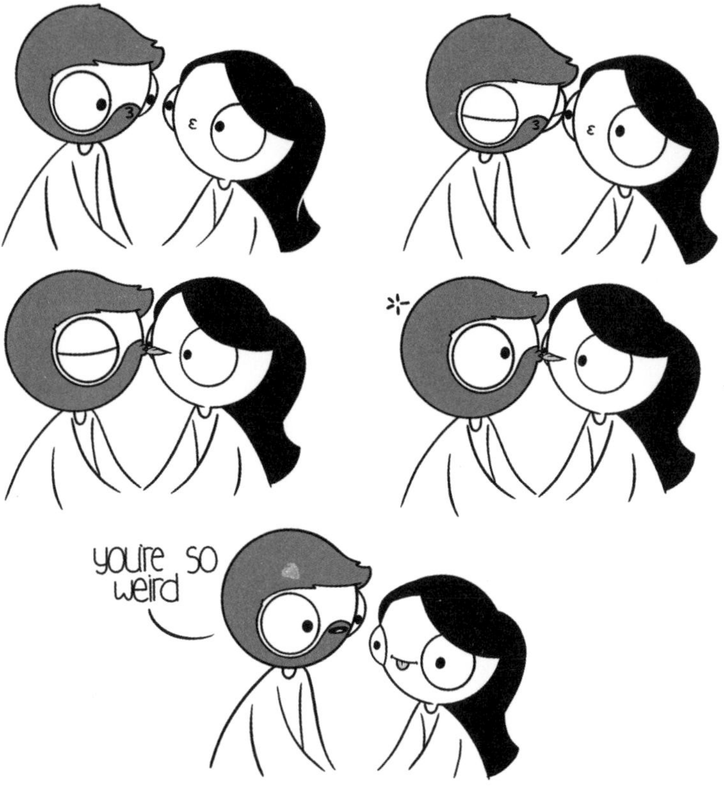
you're so weird

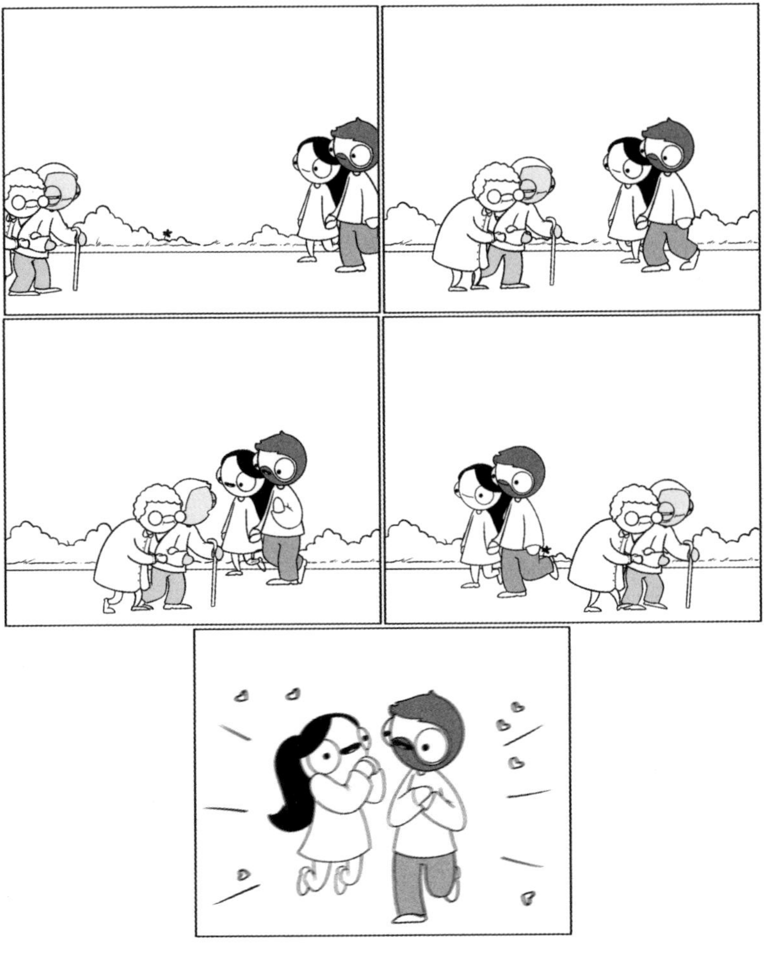

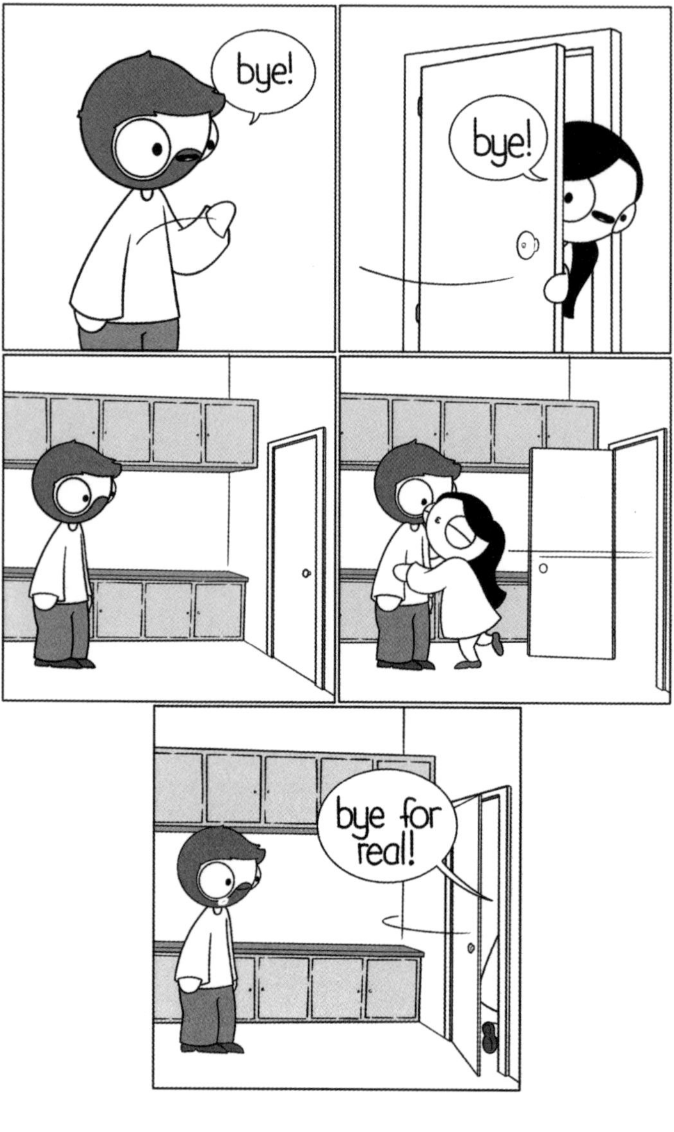
bye!
bye!
bye for real!

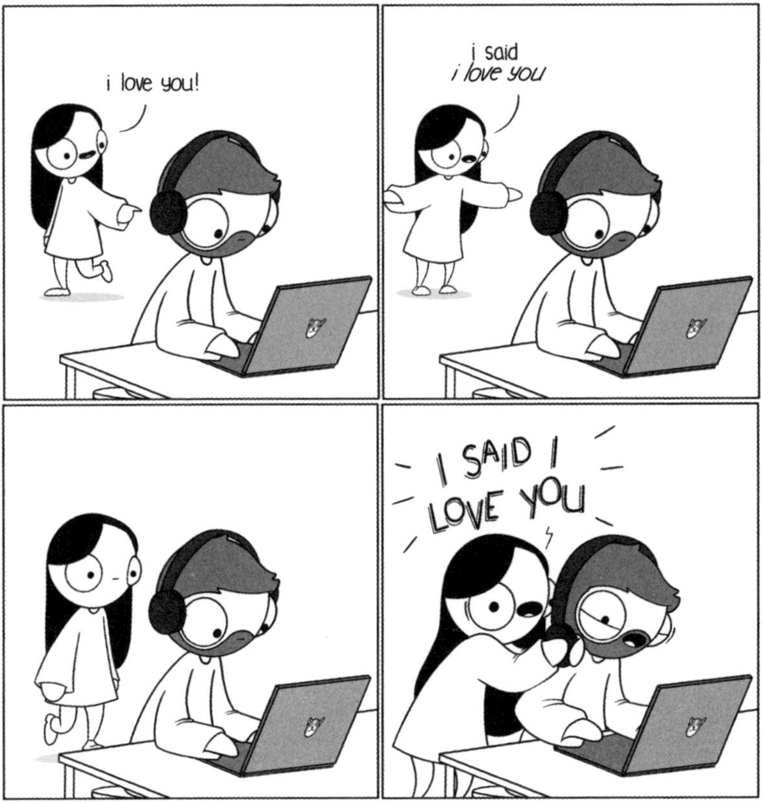
i love you!
i said
*i love you*
I SAID I
LOVE YOU

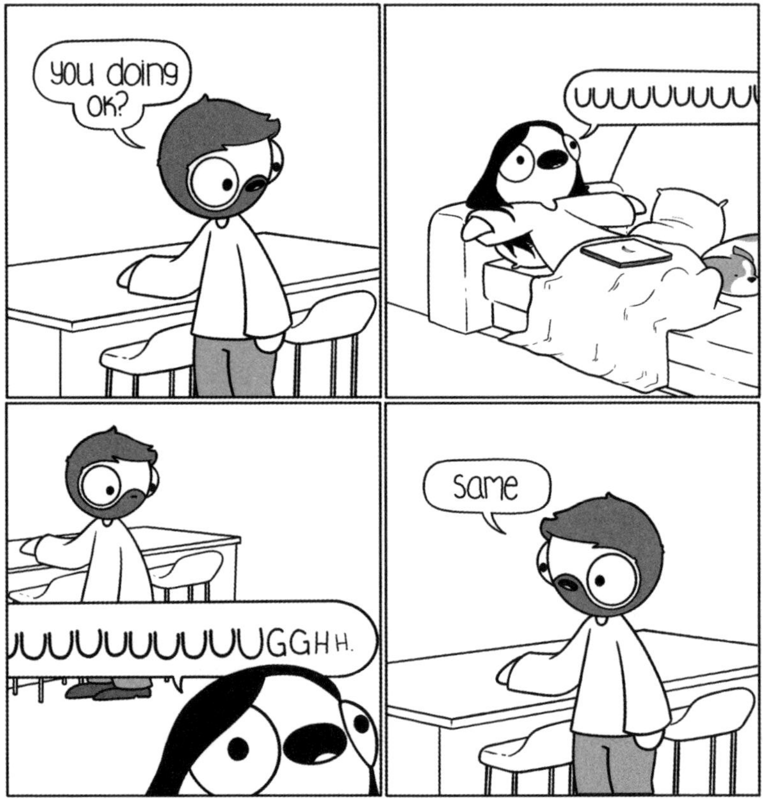
you doing ok?
UUUUUUUUU
UUUUUUUUUUGGHH.
same

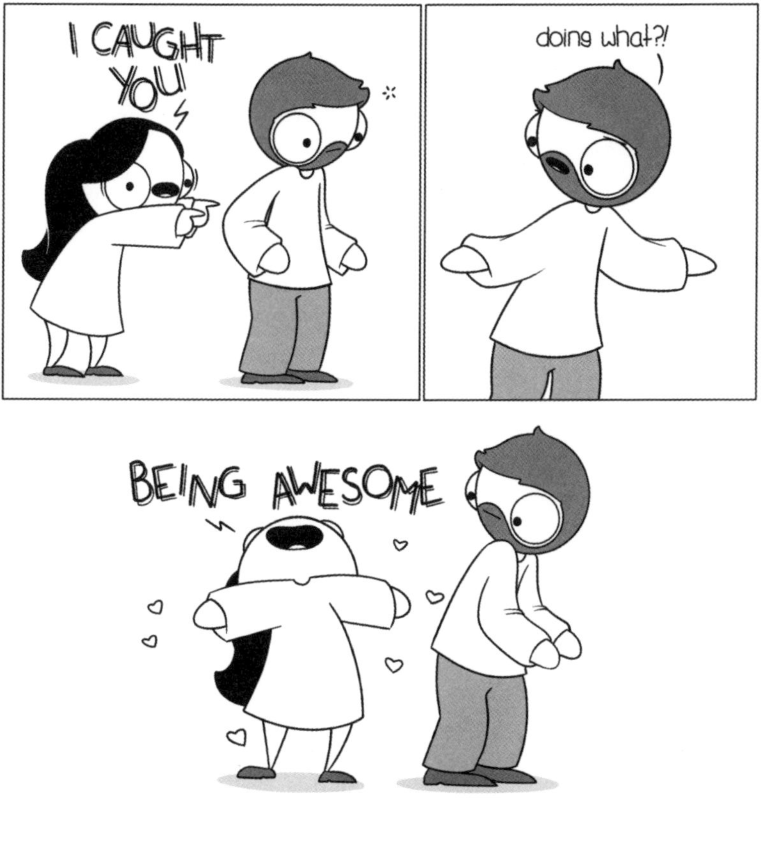
I CAUGHT YOU!
doing what?!
BEING AWESOME

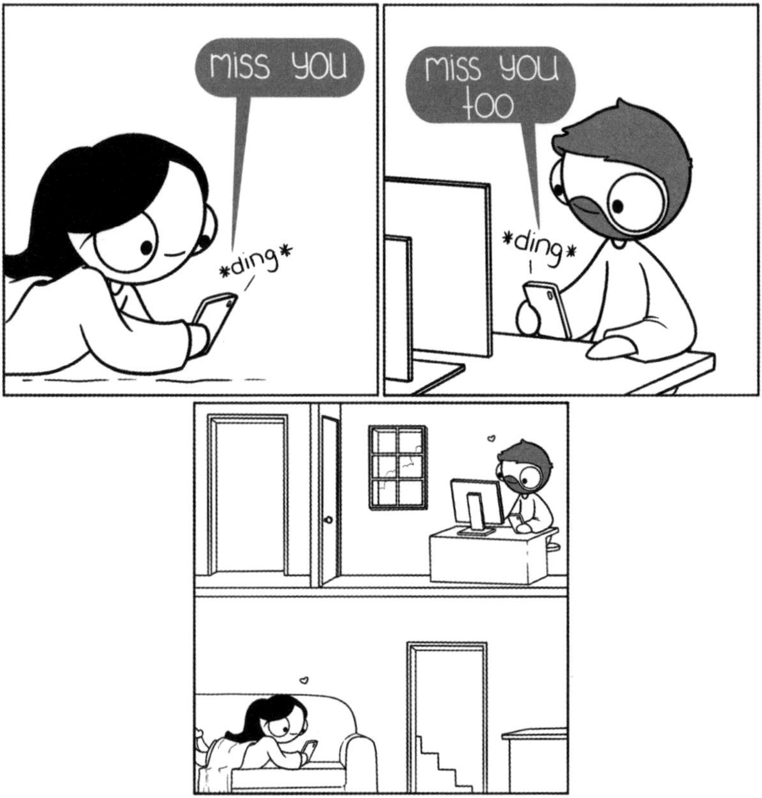
MISS YOU
*ding*
MISS YOU TOO
*ding*

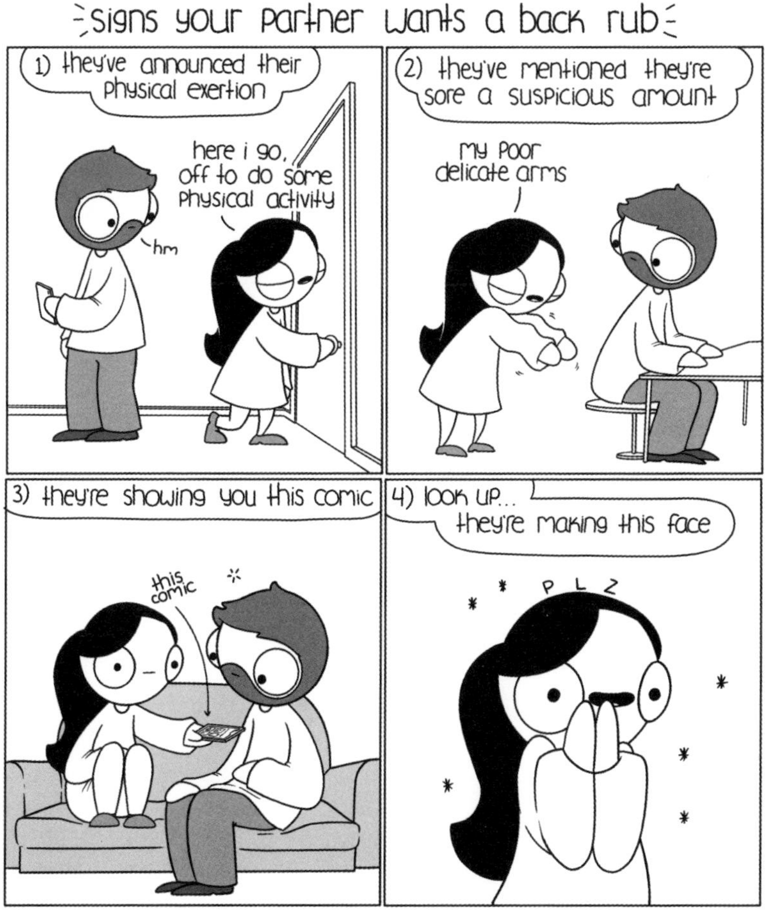

signs your partner wants a back rub
1) they've announced their physical exertion
here i go, off to do some physical activity
hm
2) they've mentioned they're sore a suspicious amount
my poor delicate arms
3) they're showing you this comic
this comic
4) look up... they're making this face
P L Z

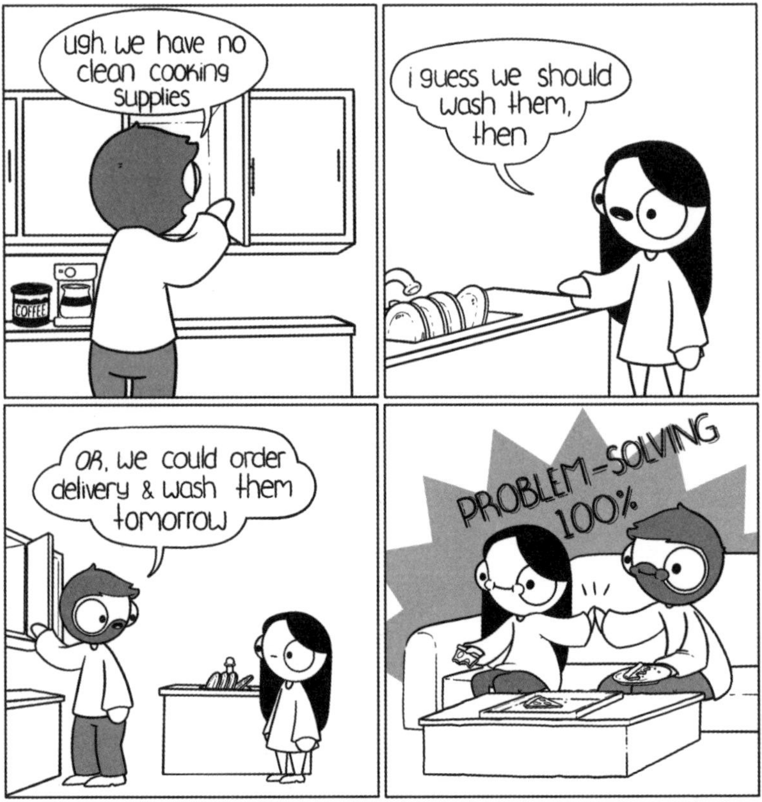
ugh. we have no clean cooking supplies
i guess we should wash them, then
OR, we could order delivery & wash them tomorrow
COFFEE
PROBLEM-SOLVING 100%

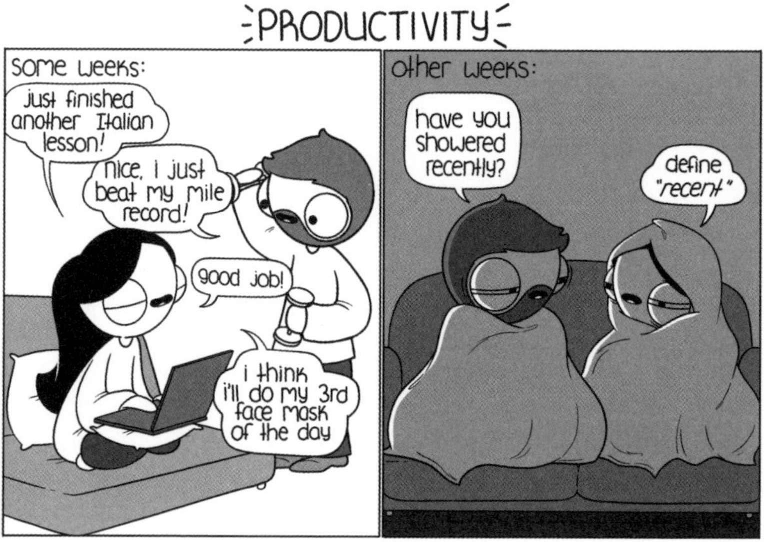
PRODUCTIVITY
some weeks:
just finished another Italian lesson!
nice, i just beat my mile record!
good job!
i think i'll do my 3rd face mask of the day
other weeks:
have you showered recently?
define "recent"

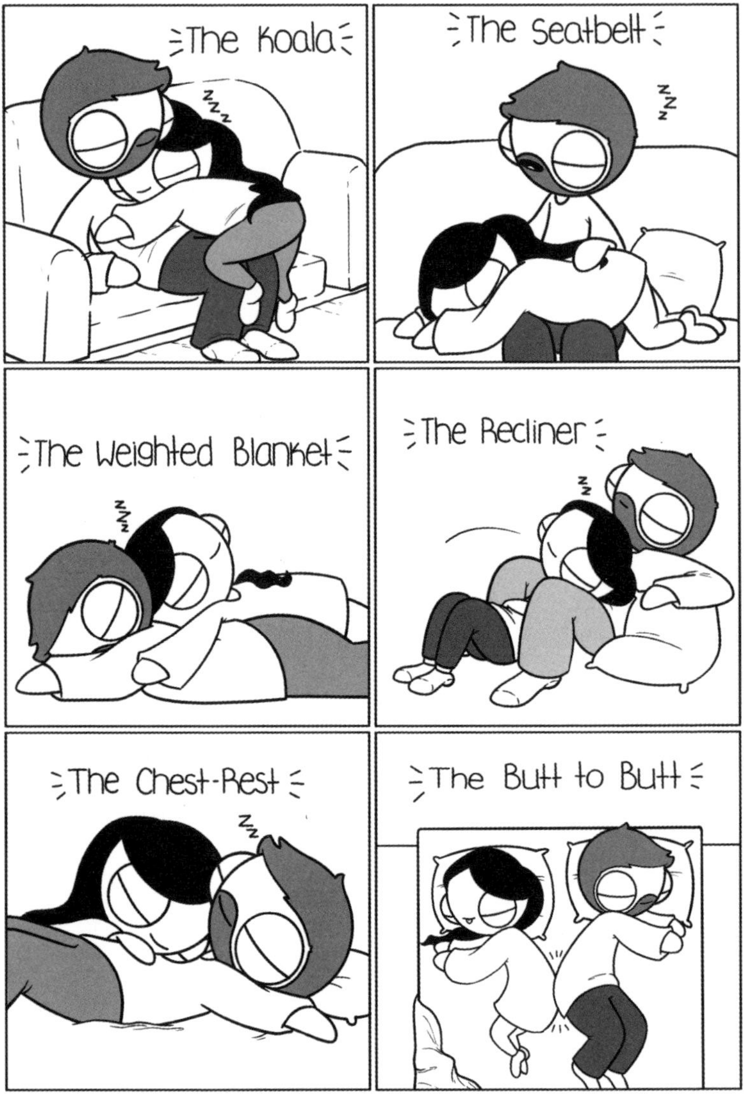
The Koala
ZZZ
The Seatbelt
ZZZ
The Weighted Blanket
ZZZ
The Recliner
ZZZ
The Chest-Rest
ZZ
The Butt to Butt

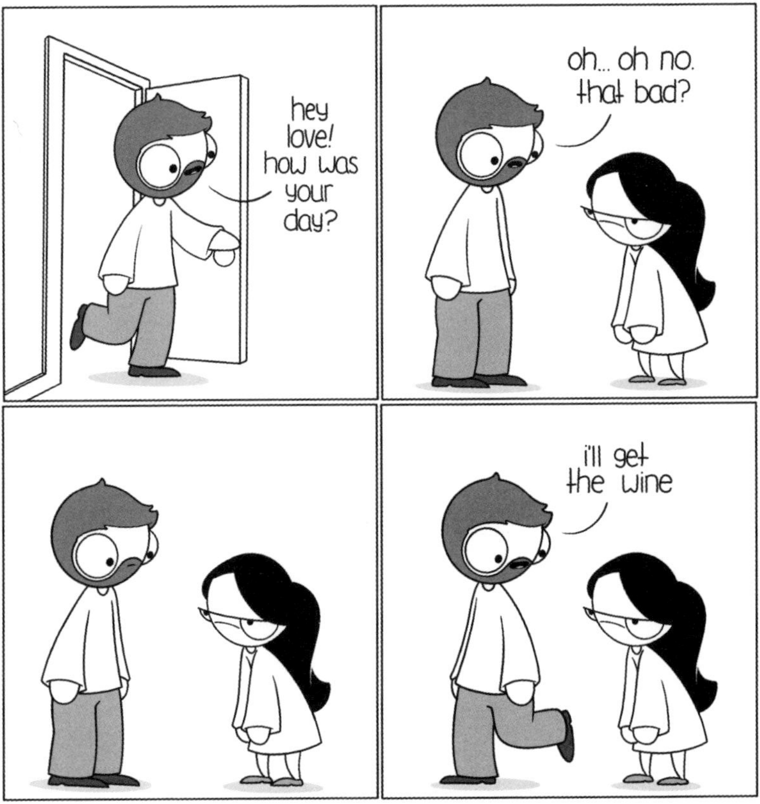
hey love! how was your day?
oh... oh no. that bad?
i'll get the wine

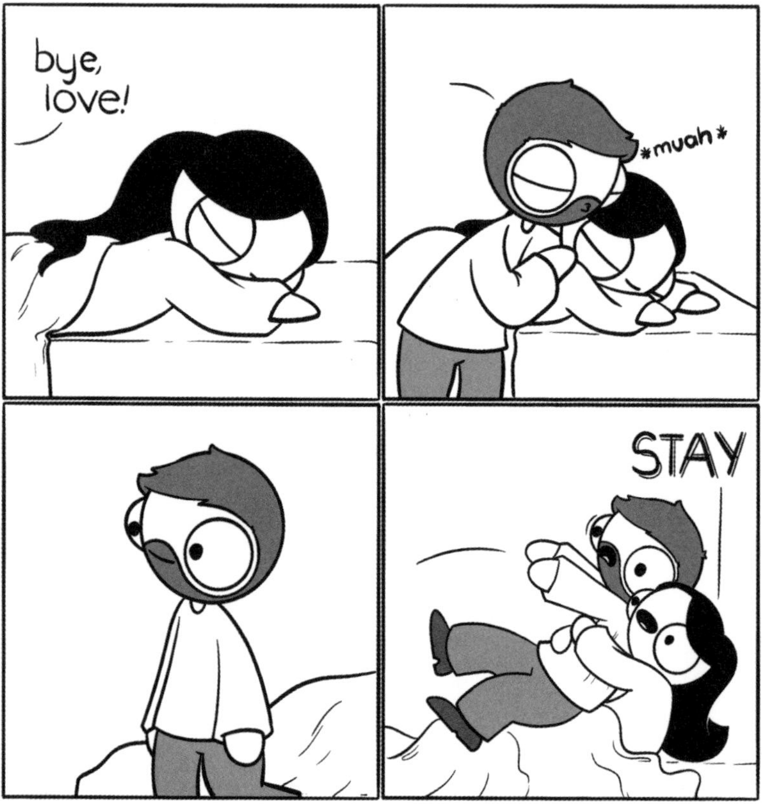
bye,
love!
*muah*
STAY

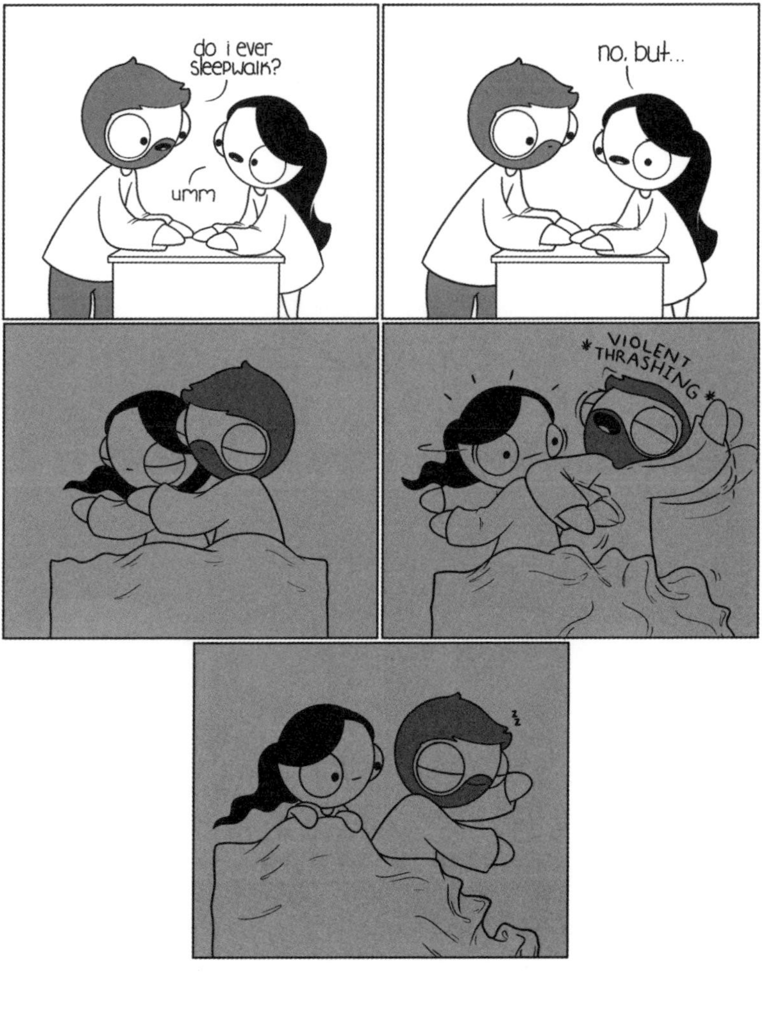
do i ever sleepwalk?
umm
no, but...
*VIOLENT THRASHING*
z z

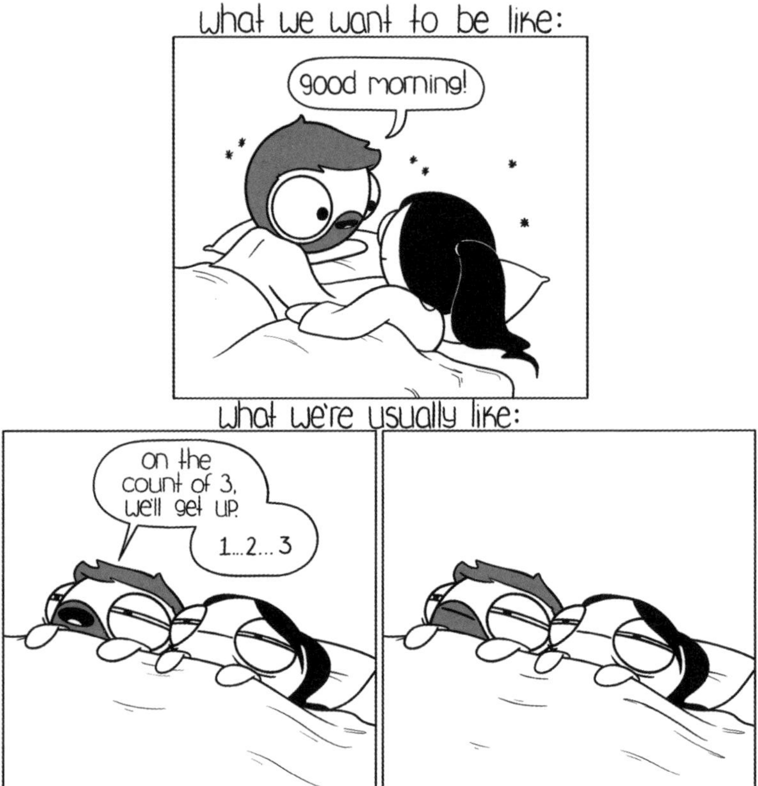
what we want to be like:
good morning!
what we're usually like:
on the count of 3, we'll get up.
1...2...3

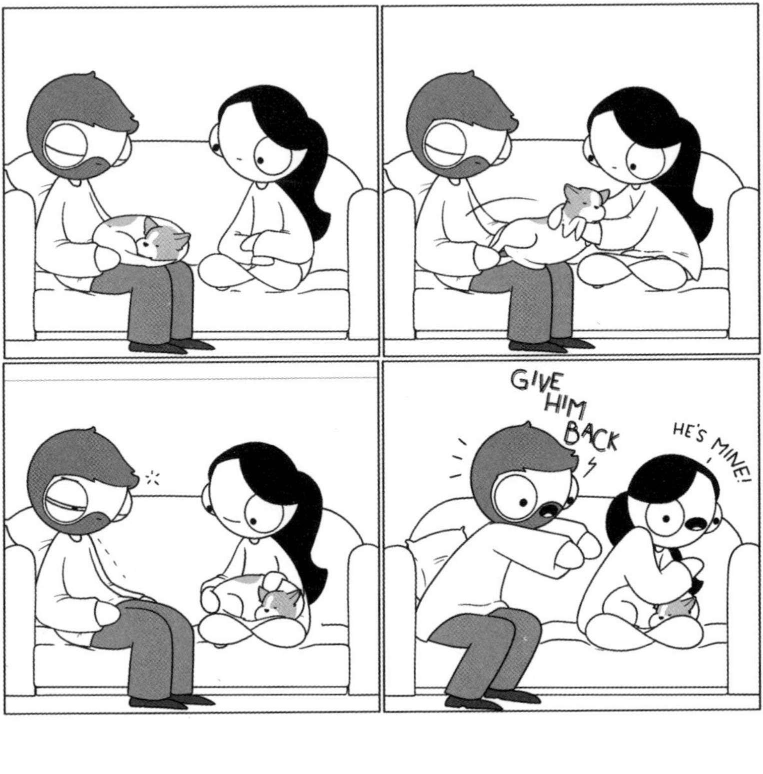
GIVE HIM BACK
HE'S MINE!

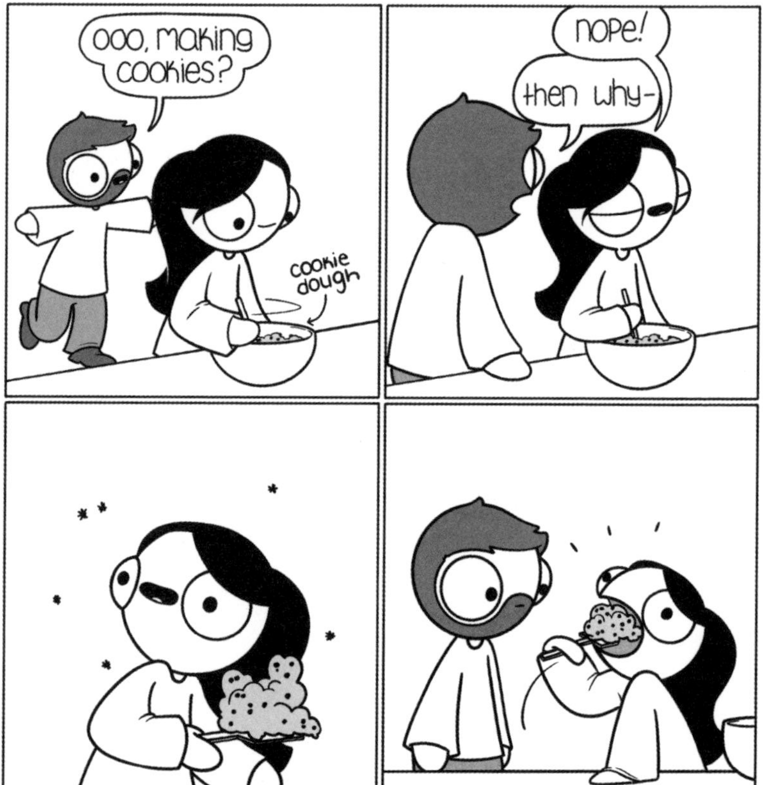
ooo, making cookies?
cookie dough
nope!
then why-

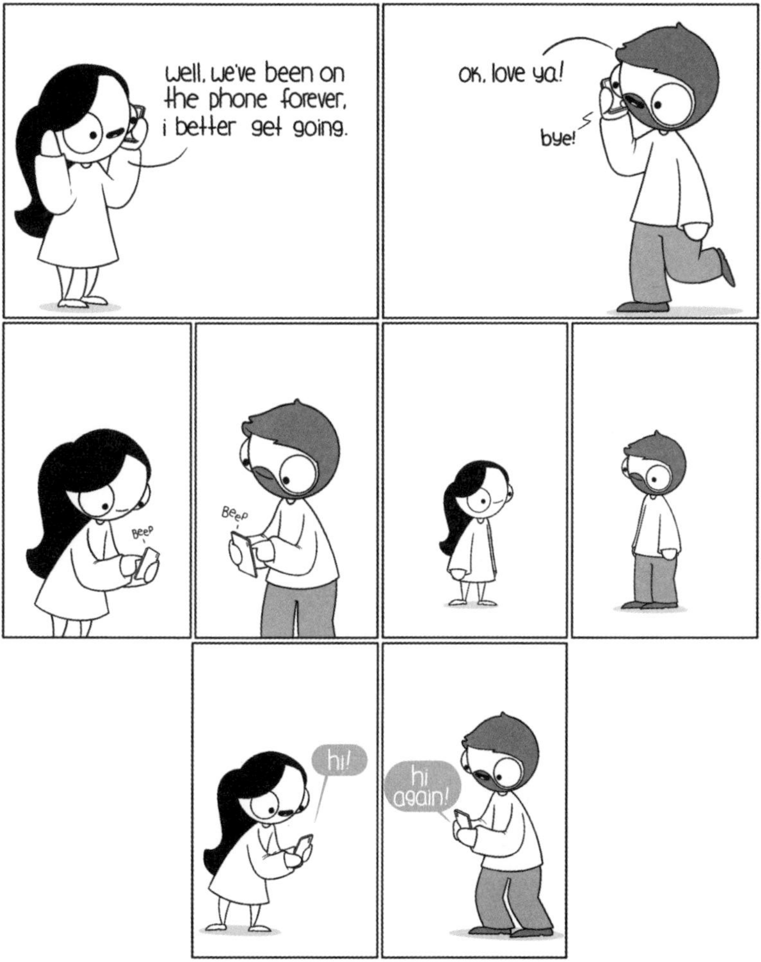
well, we've been on the phone forever, i better get going.
ok, love ya!
bye!
Beep
Beep
hi!
hi again!

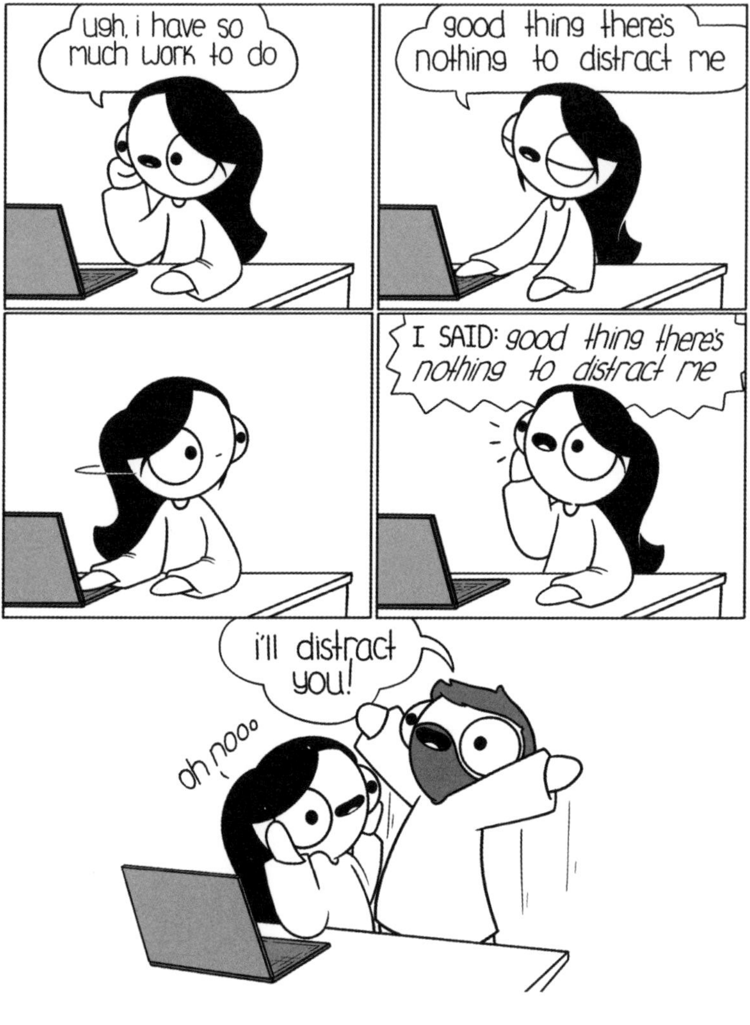
ugh, i have so much work to do
good thing there's nothing to distract me
I SAID: good thing there's nothing to distract me
i'll distract you!
oh nooo

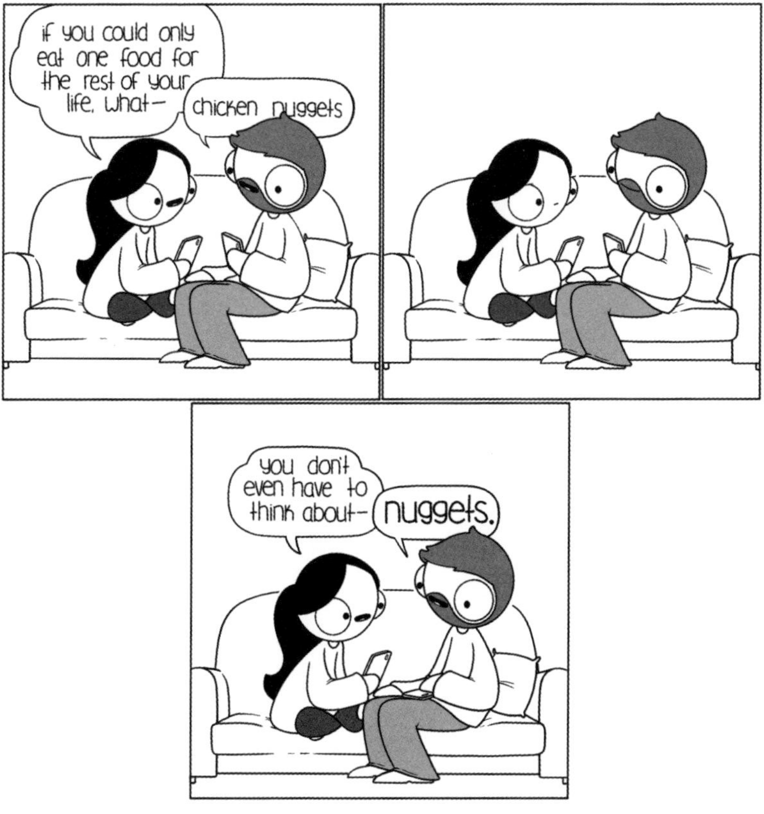
if you could only eat one food for the rest of your life, what-
chicken nuggets
you don't even have to think about-
nuggets.

# working from home

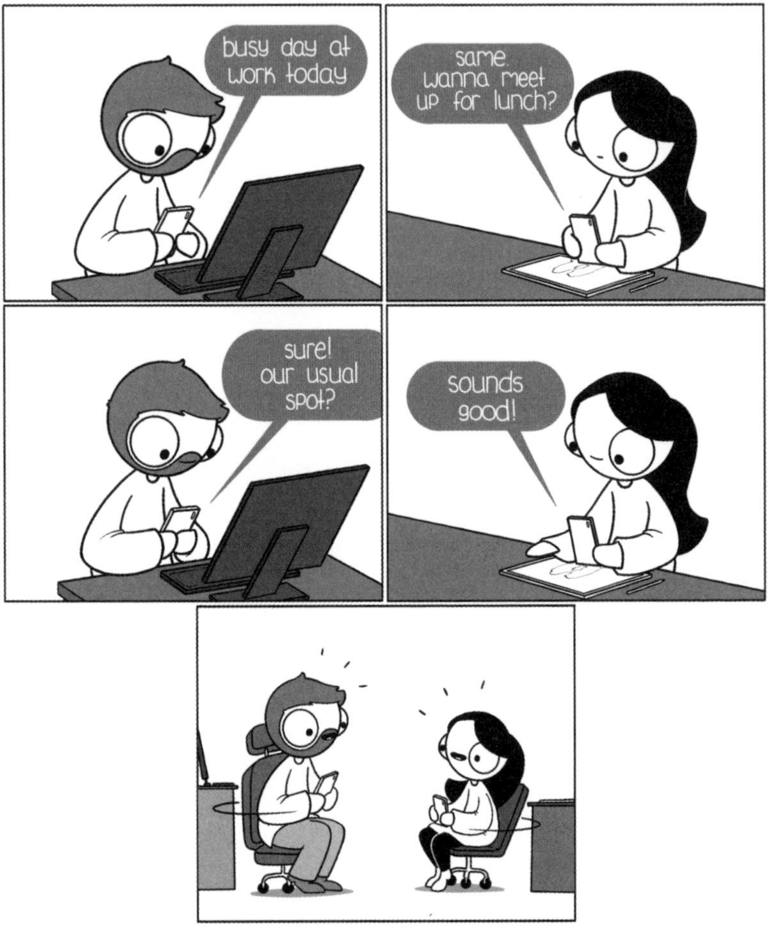
busy day at work today
same. wanna meet up for lunch?
sure! our usual spot?
sounds good!

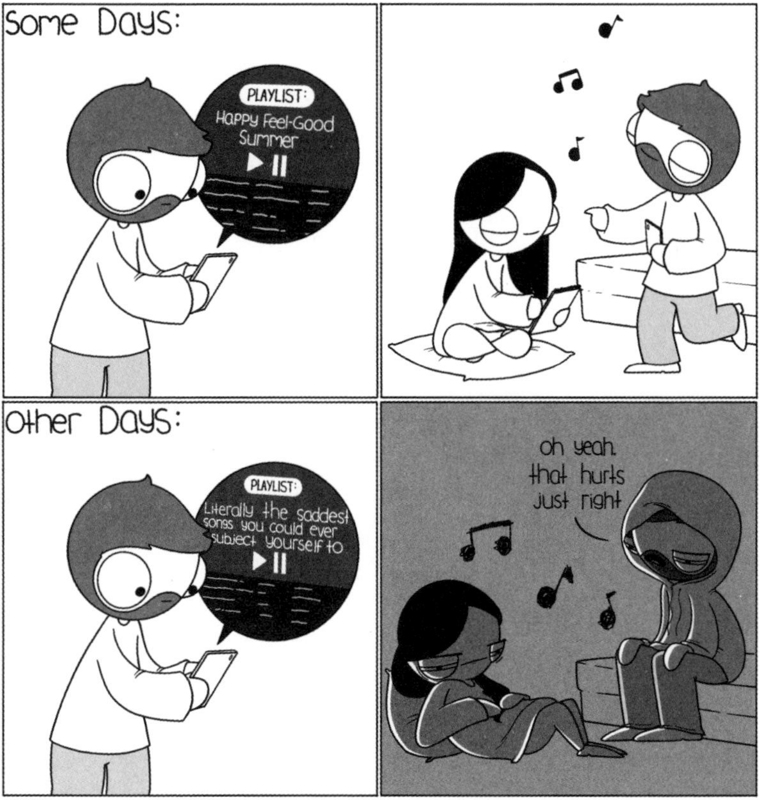
Some Days:
PLAYLIST:
Happy Feel-Good Summer
Other Days:
PLAYLIST:
Literally the saddest songs you could ever subject yourself to
oh yeah. that hurts just right

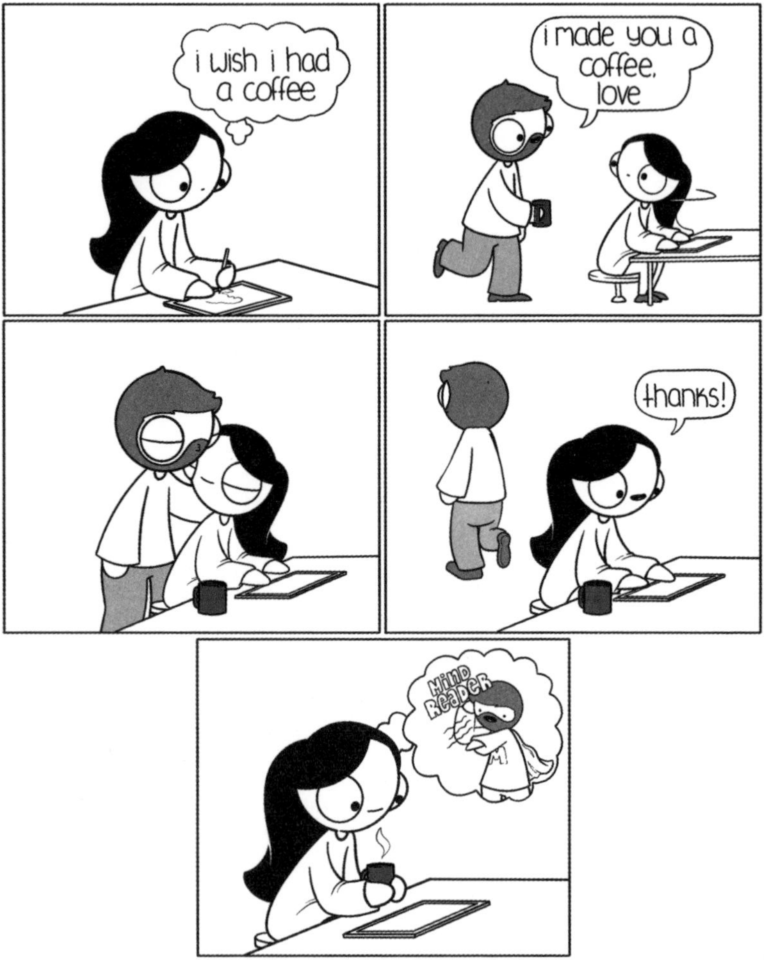
i wish i had a coffee
i made you a coffee, love
thanks!
MIND READER

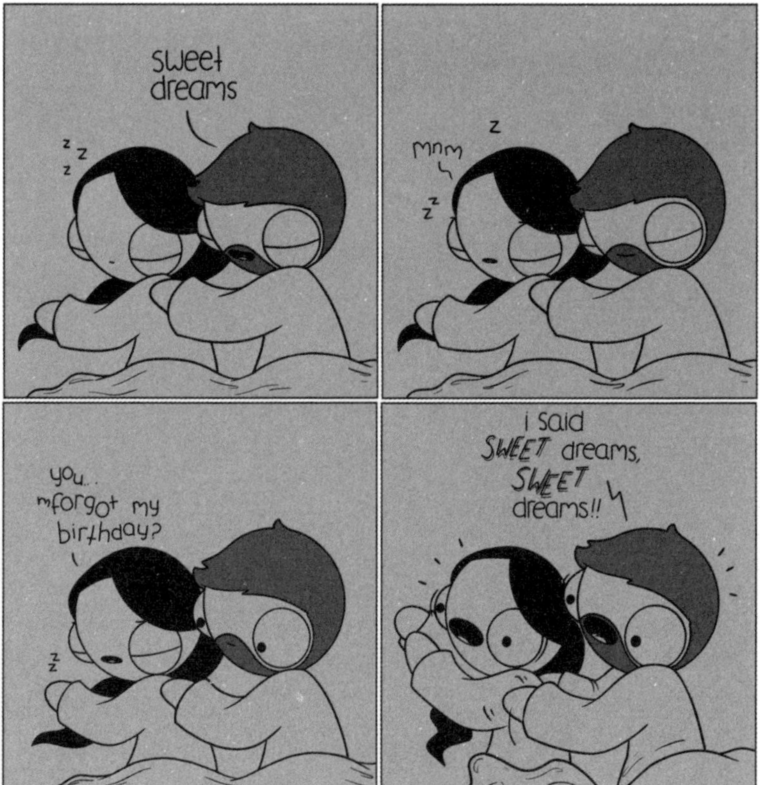
sweet dreams
z z z
z
mnm
z z
you... mforgot my birthday?
z z
i said SWEET dreams, SWEET dreams!!

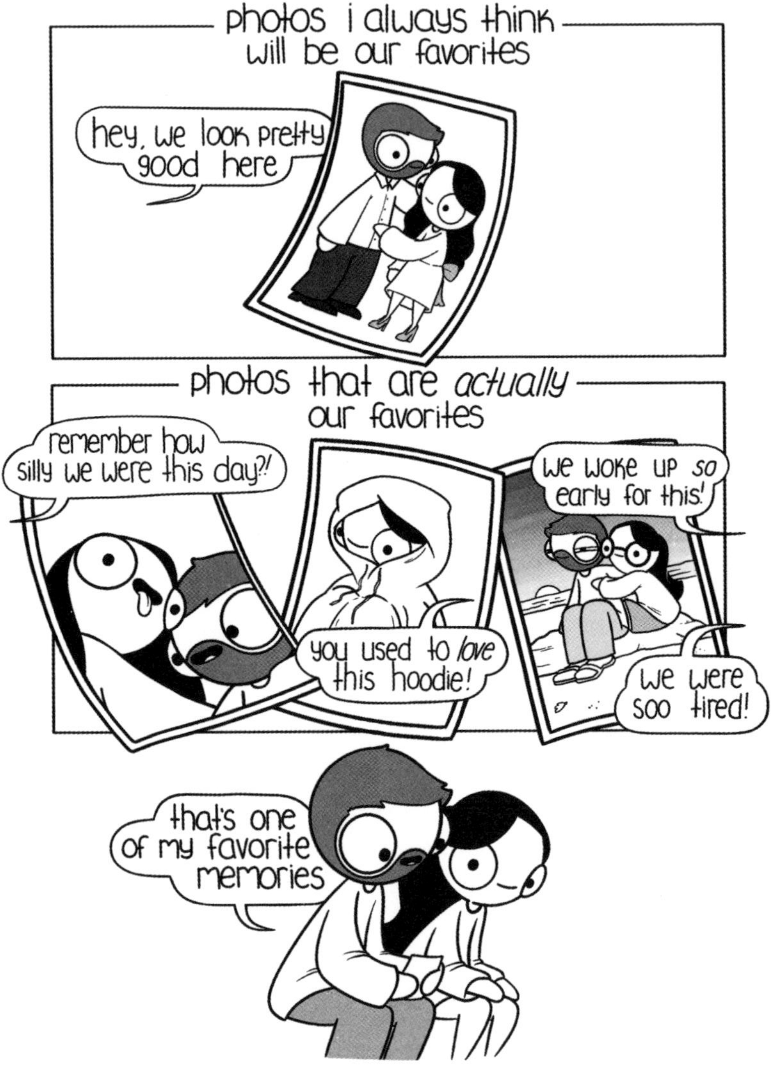
photos i always think will be our favorites
hey, we look pretty good here
photos that are *actually* our favorites
remember how silly we were this day?!
we woke up *so* early for this!
you used to *love* this hoodie!
we were soo tired!
that's one of my favorite memories

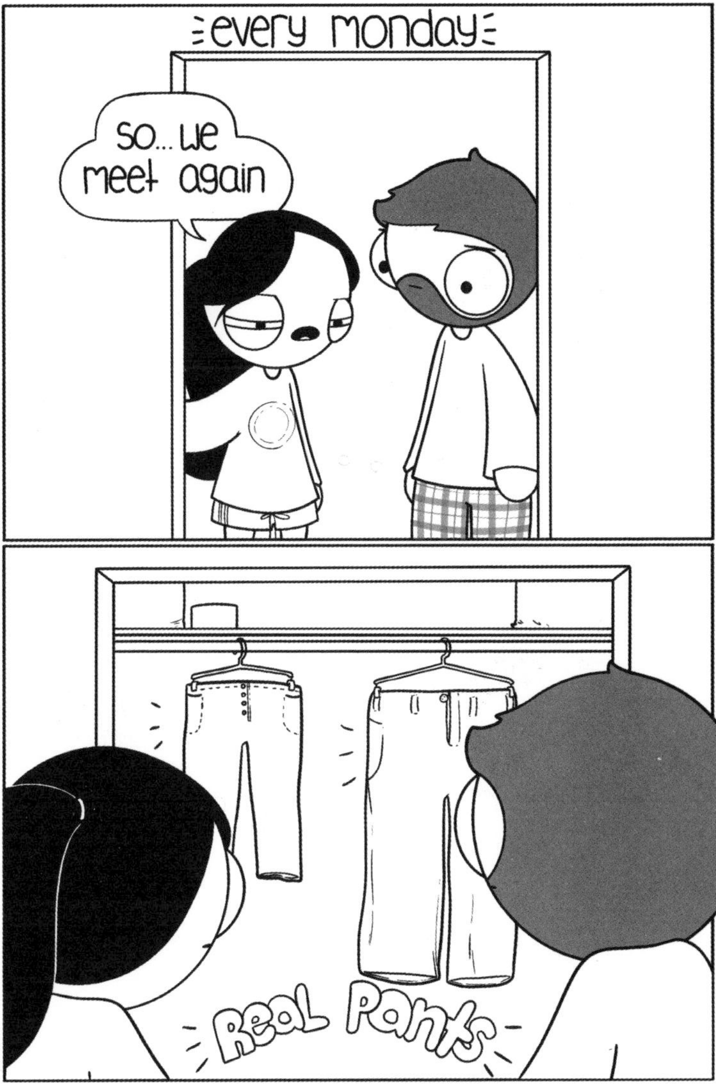
every monday
so... we meet again
Real Pants

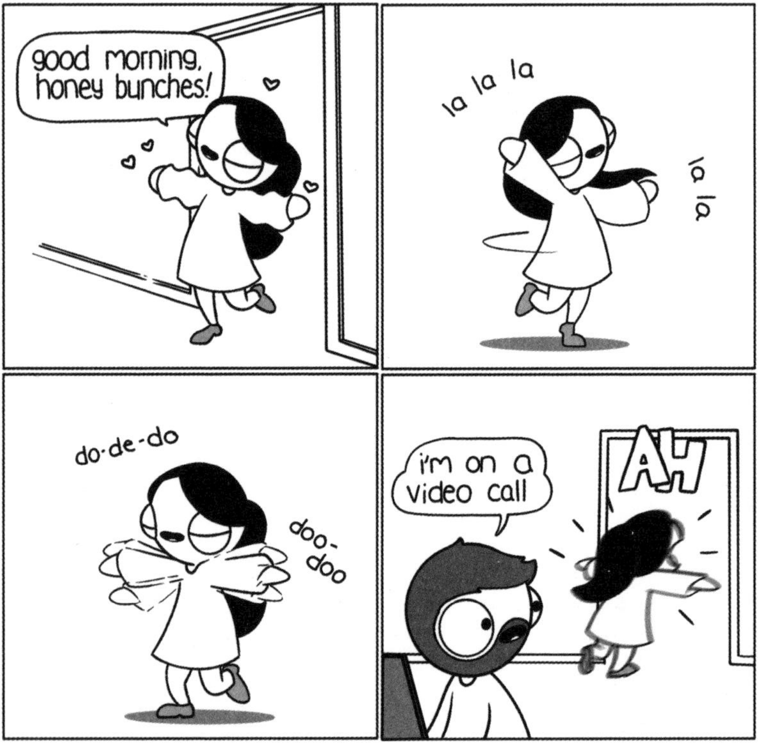
good morning, honey bunches!
la la la
la la
do-de-do
doo-doo
i'm on a video call
AH

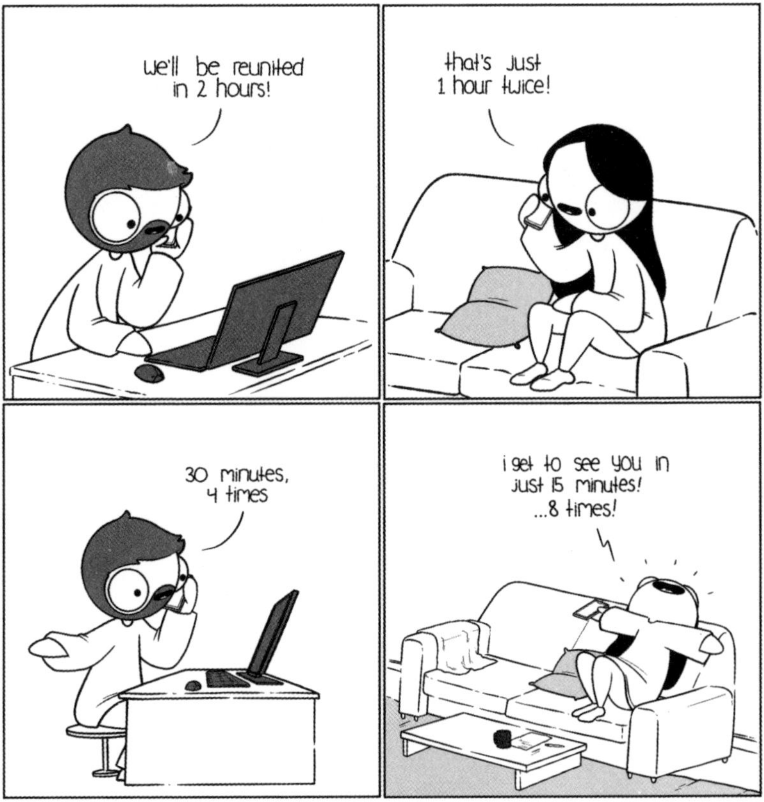
we'll be reunited in 2 hours!
that's just 1 hour twice!
30 minutes, 4 times
i get to see you in just 15 minutes! ...8 times!

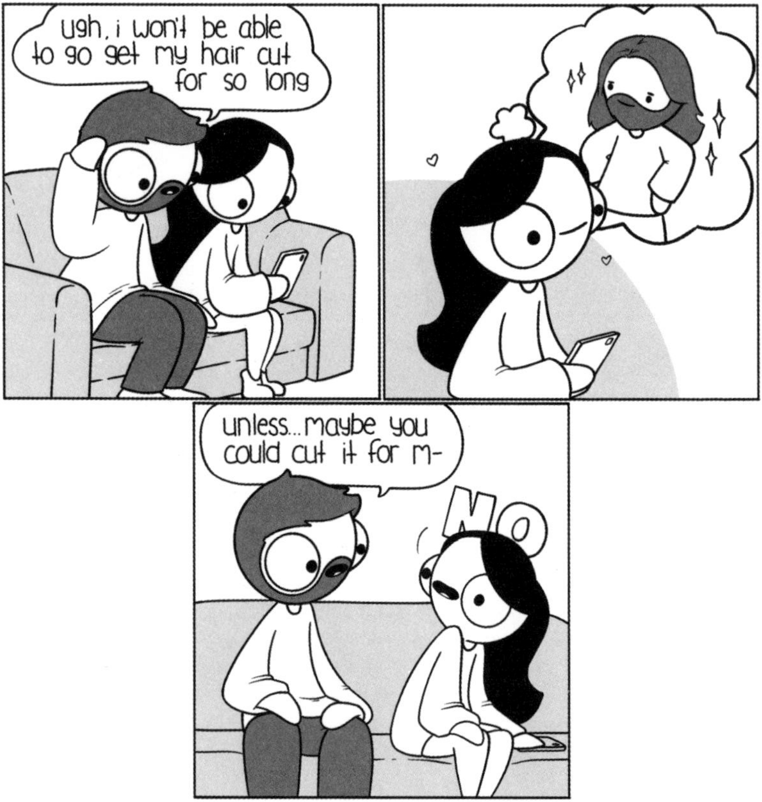
ugh, i won't be able to go get my hair cut for so long
unless...maybe you could cut it for m-
NO

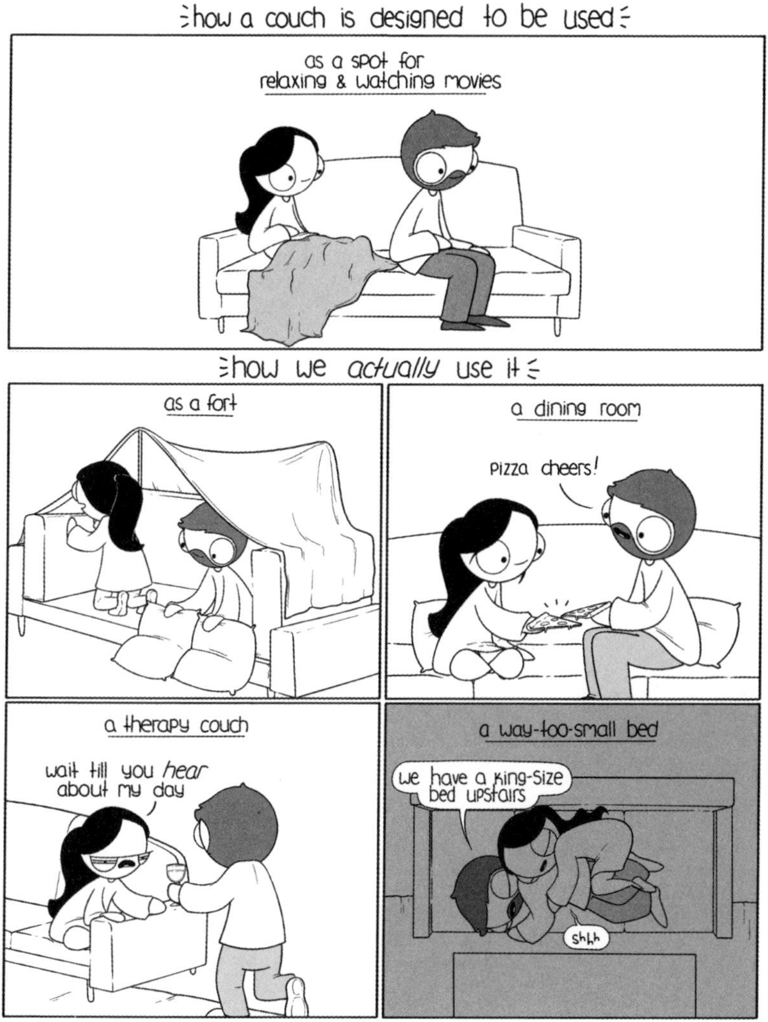
how a couch is designed to be used
as a spot for relaxing & watching movies
how we *actually* use it
as a fort
a dining room
pizza cheers!
a therapy couch
wait till you *hear* about my day
a way-too-small bed
we have a king-size bed upstairs
shhh

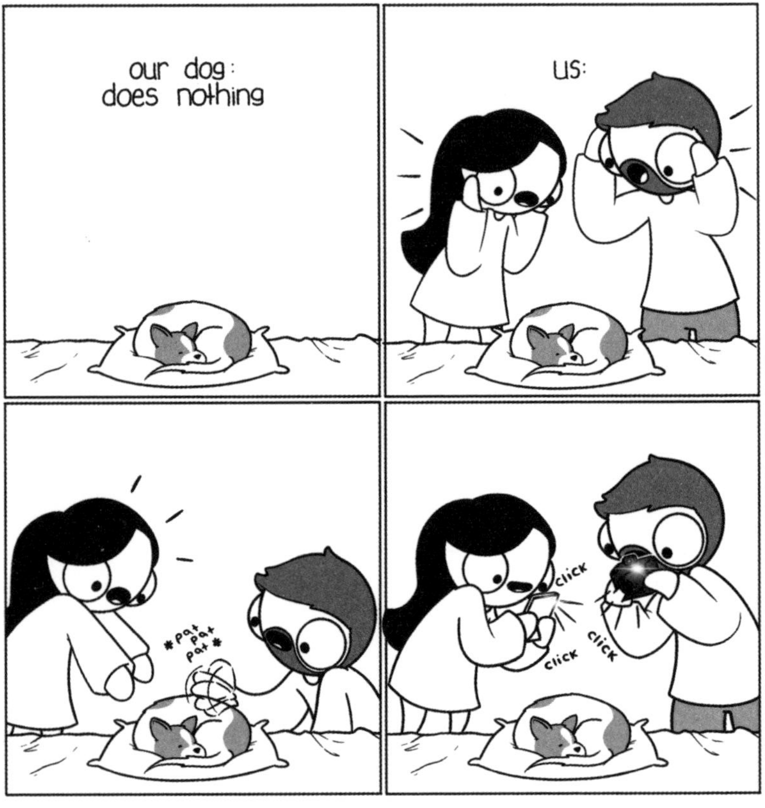
our dog:
does nothing
us:
*pat pat pat*
click
click
click
click

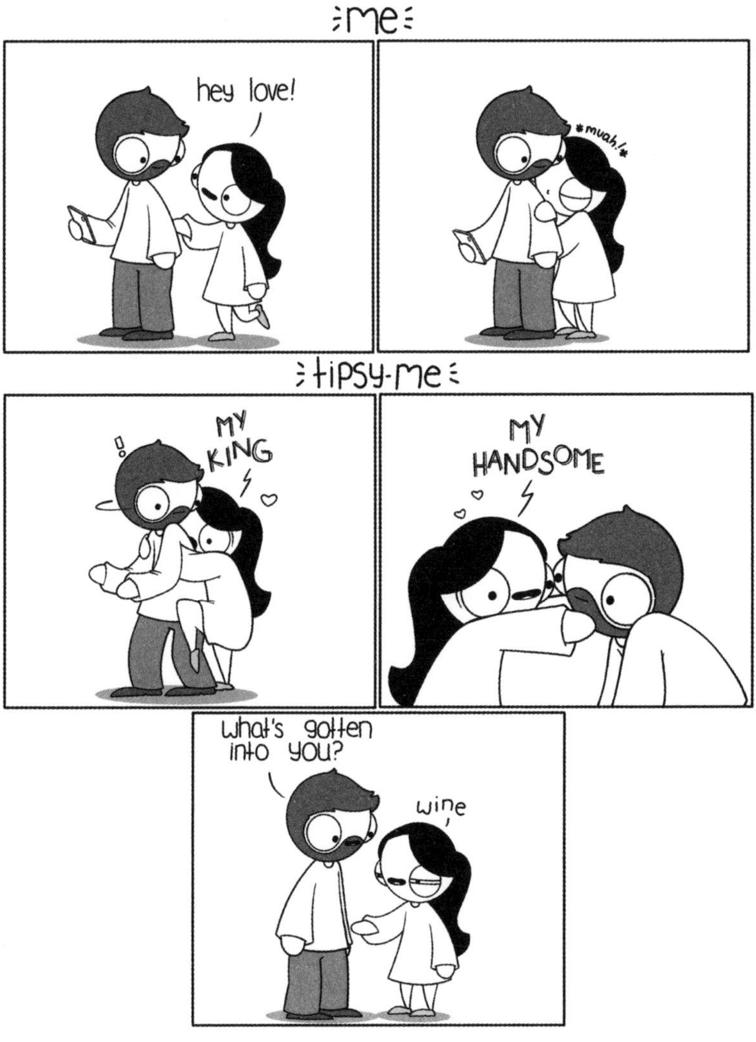
me
hey love!
*muah!*
tipsy-me
MY KING
!
MY HANDSOME
what's gotten into you?
wine

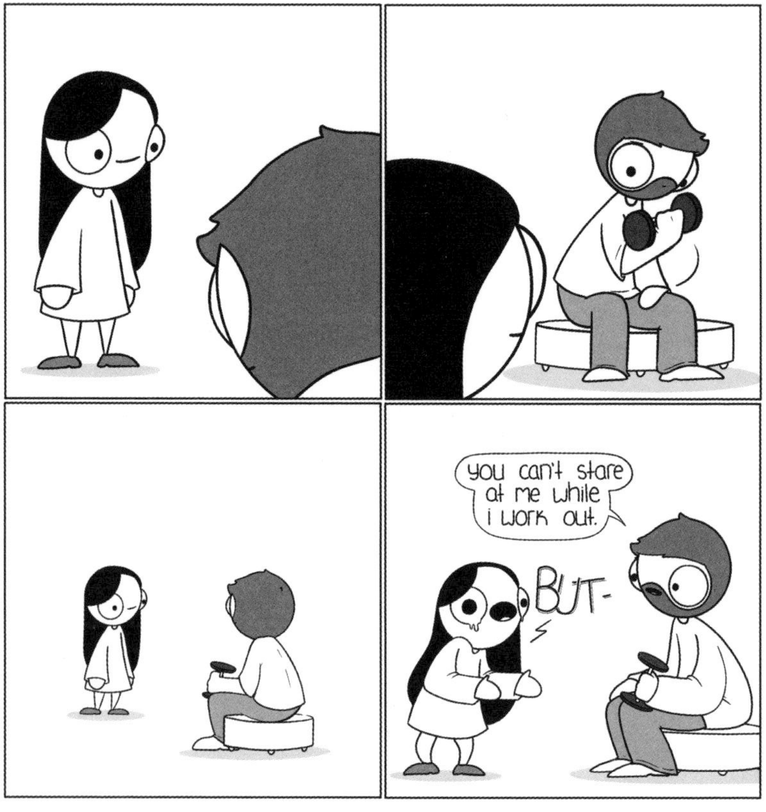
you can't stare at me while i work out.
BUT-

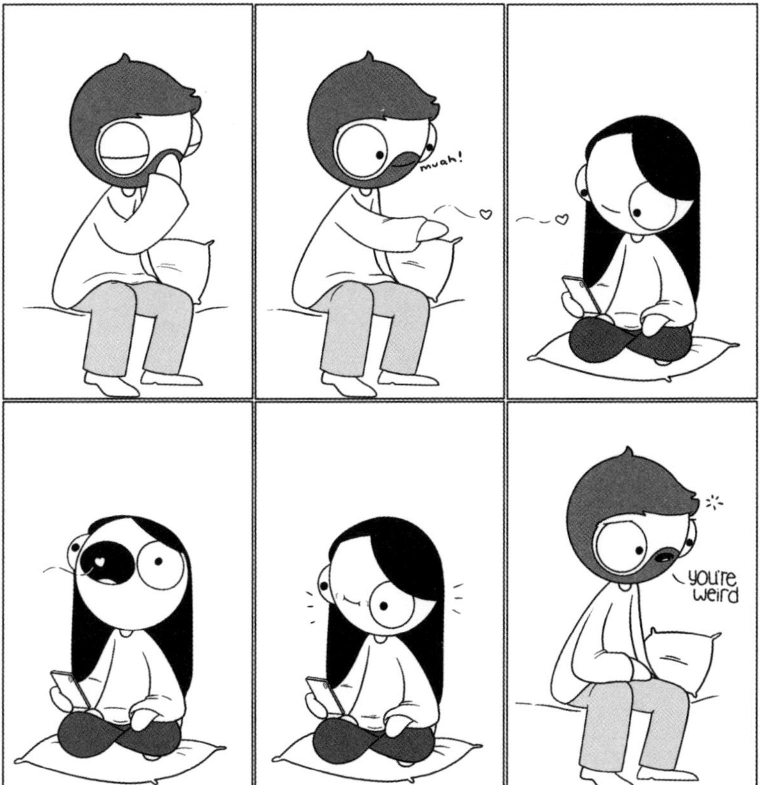
mwah!
you're weird

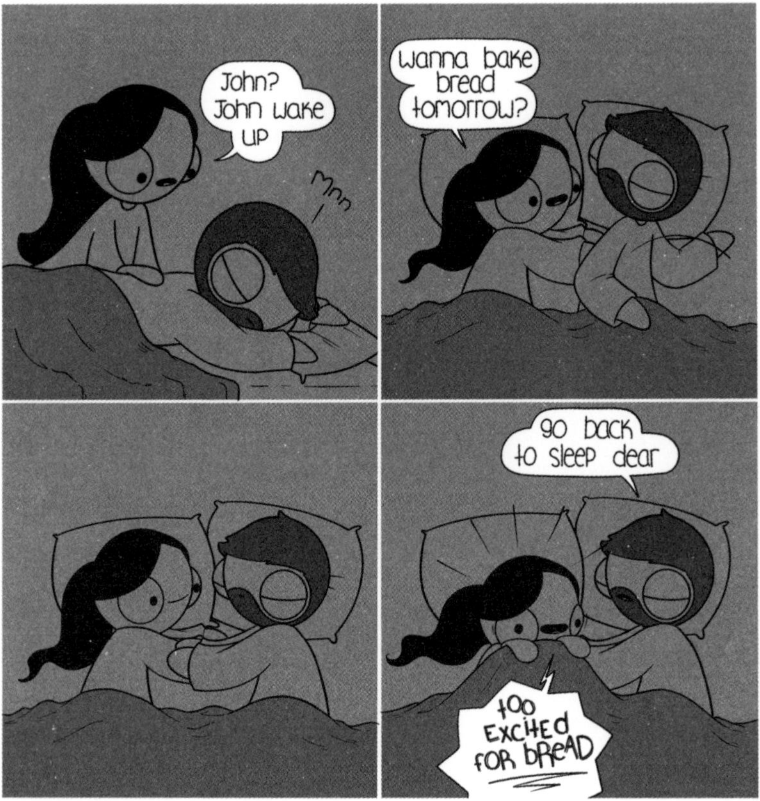
John?
John wake
up
Mnn
wanna bake
bread
tomorrow?
go back
to sleep dear
too
Excited
for bread

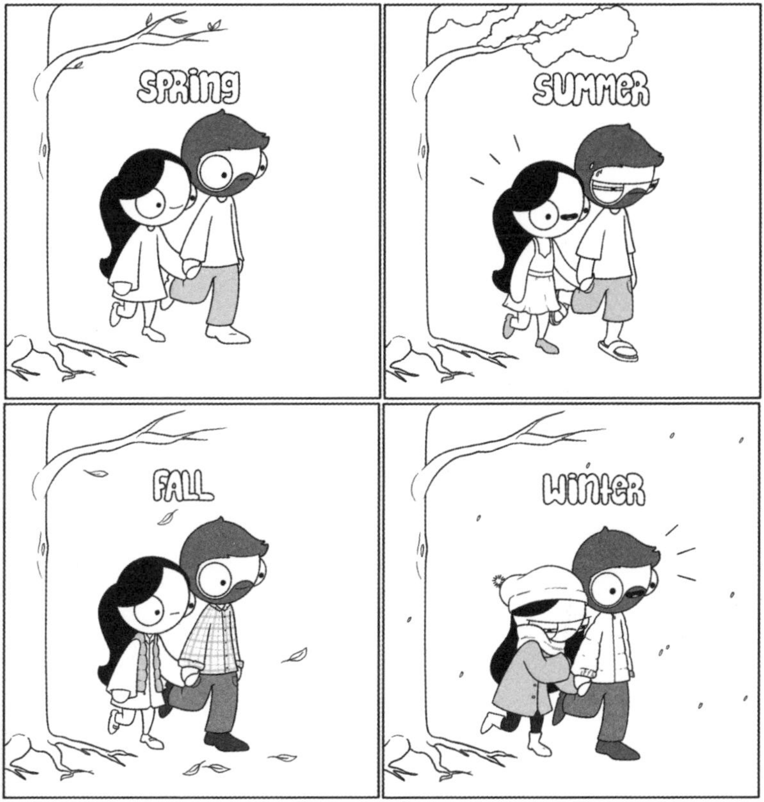
SPRING
SUMMER
FALL
WINTER

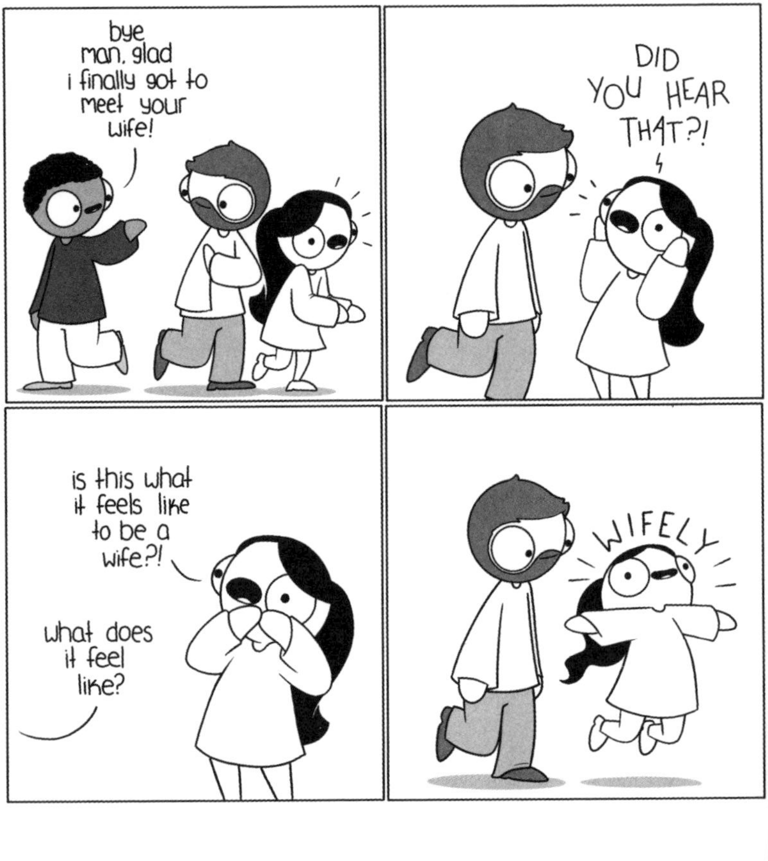
bye man, glad i finally got to meet your wife!
DID YOU HEAR THAT?!
is this what it feels like to be a wife?!
what does it feel like?
WIFELY

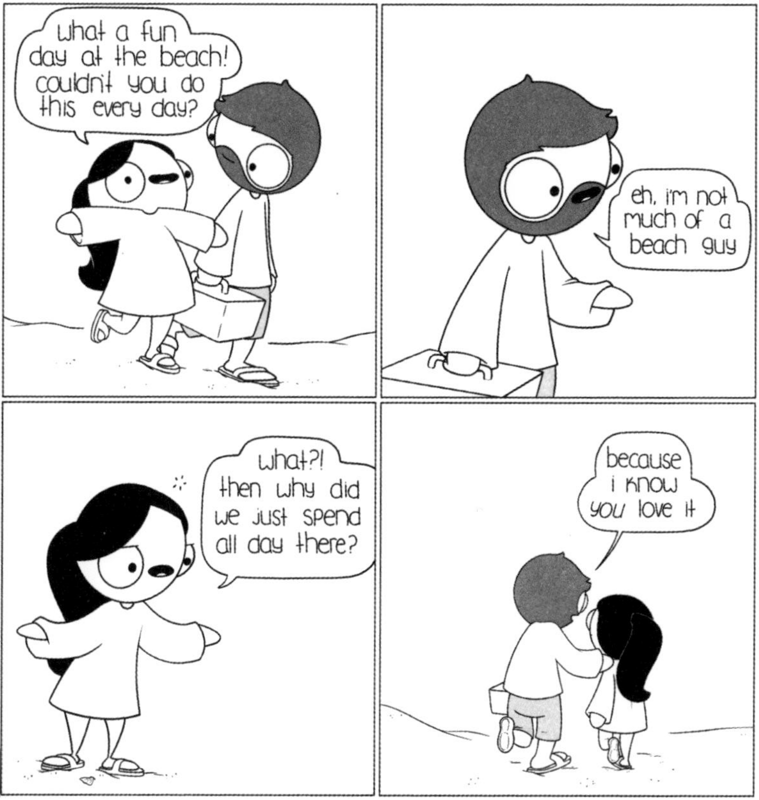
what a fun day at the beach! couldn't you do this every day?
eh, i'm not much of a beach guy
what?! then why did we just spend all day there?
because i know *you* love it

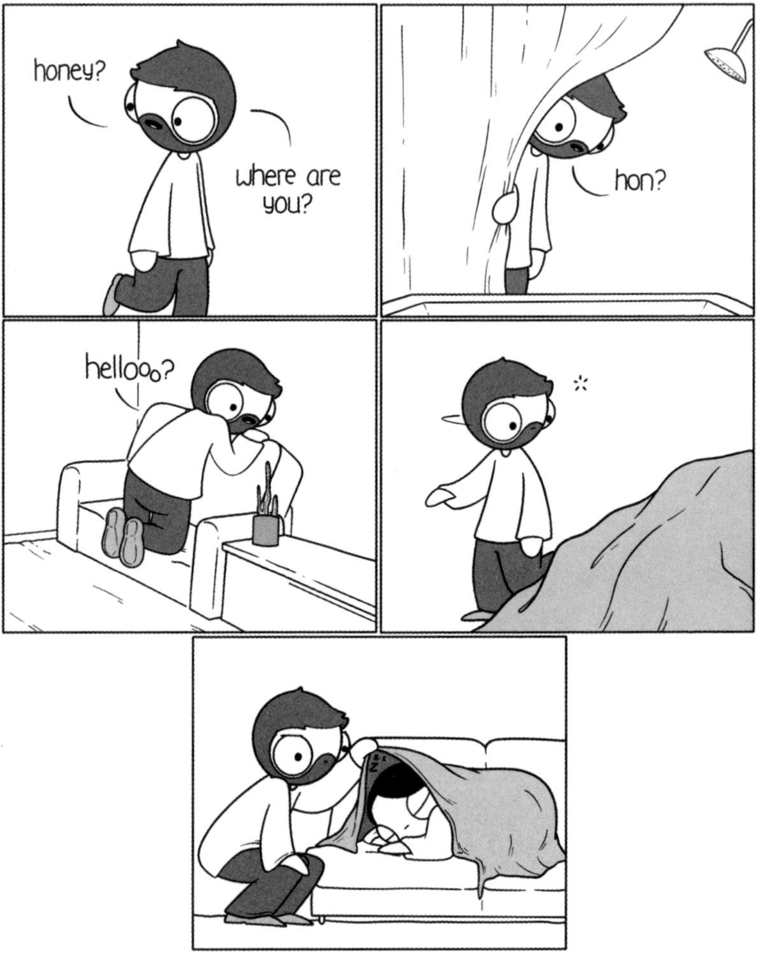
honey?
where are you?
hon?
hellooo?

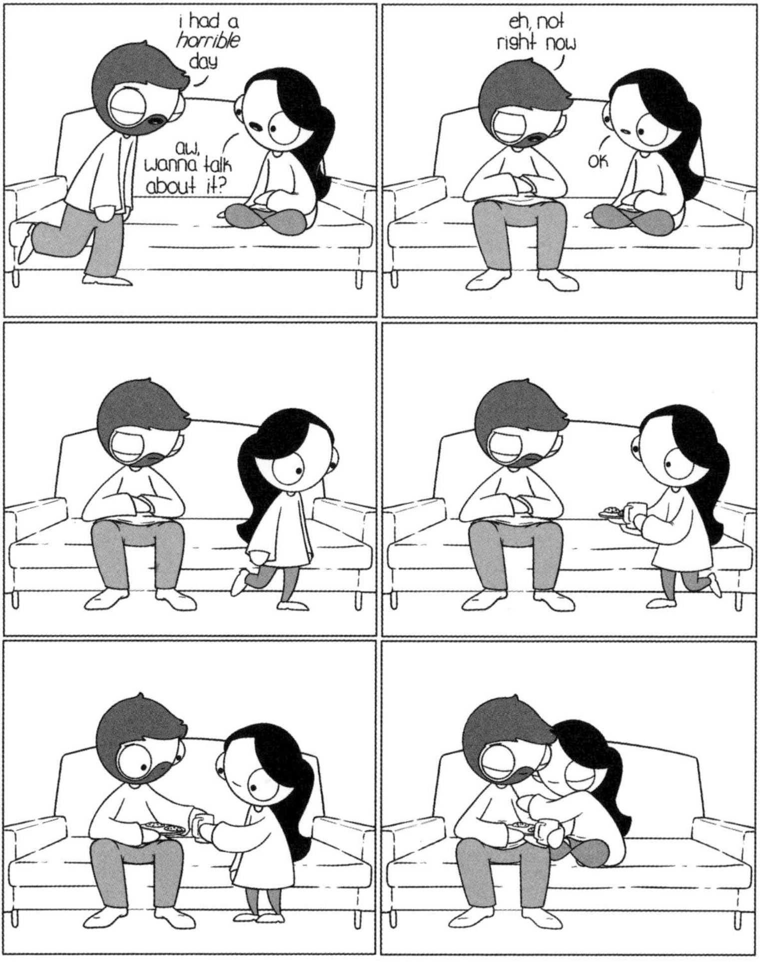
i had a *horrible* day
aw, wanna talk about it?
eh, not right now
ok

# Persistence

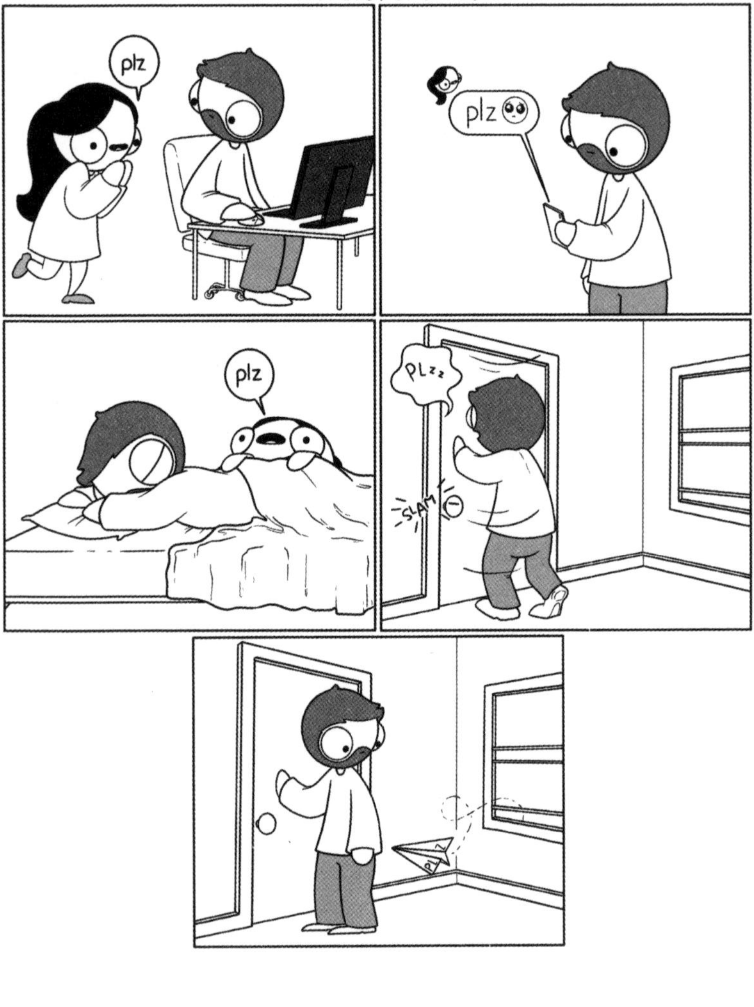
plz
plz
plz
PLzz
SLAM
PLZ

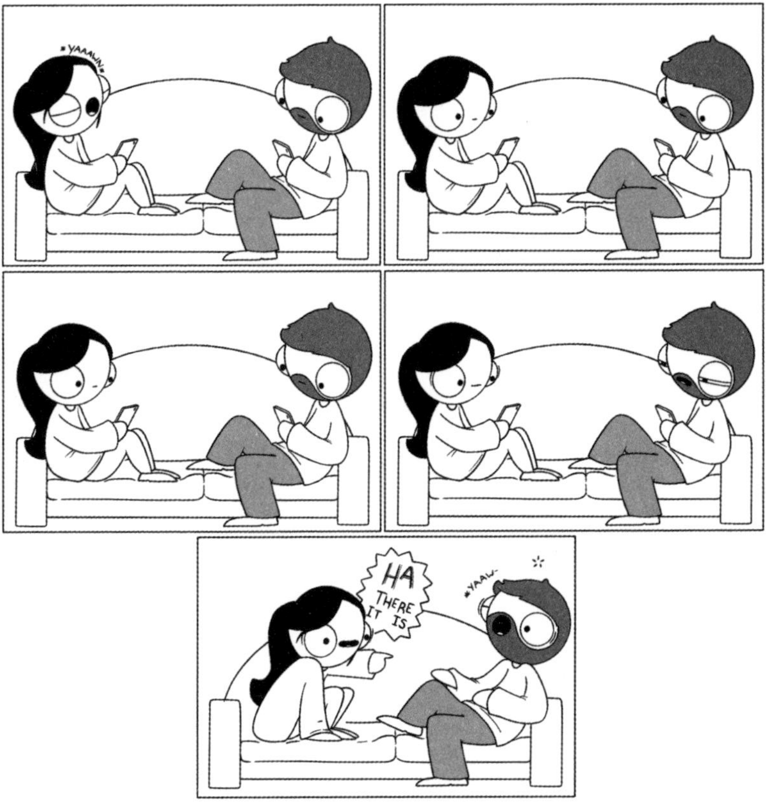
*YAAAWN*
HA
THERE IT IS
*YAAW-

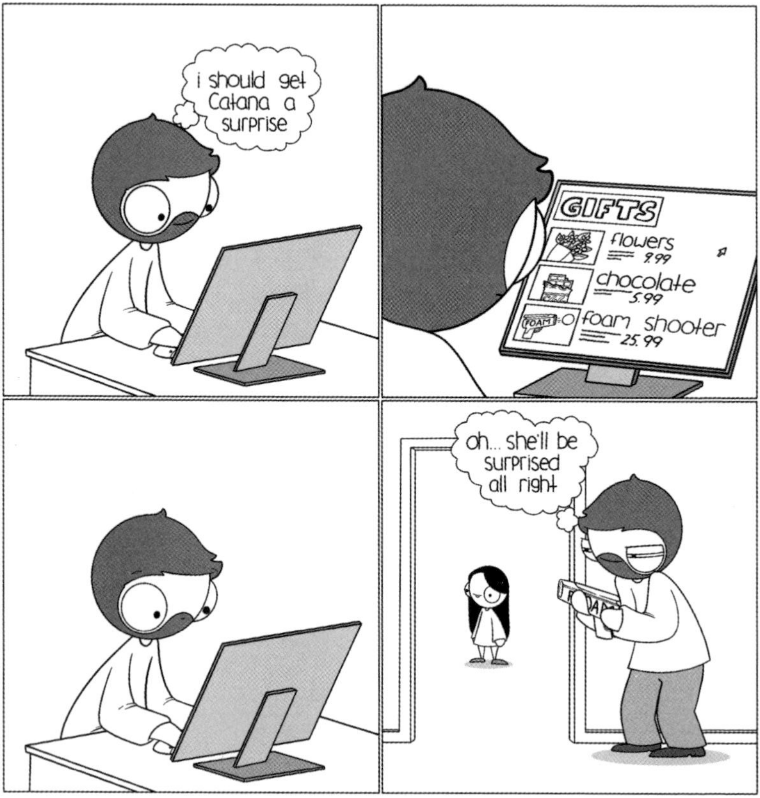
i should get Catana a surprise
GIFTS
flowers
9.99
chocolate
5.99
FOAM
foam shooter
25.99
oh... she'll be surprised all right

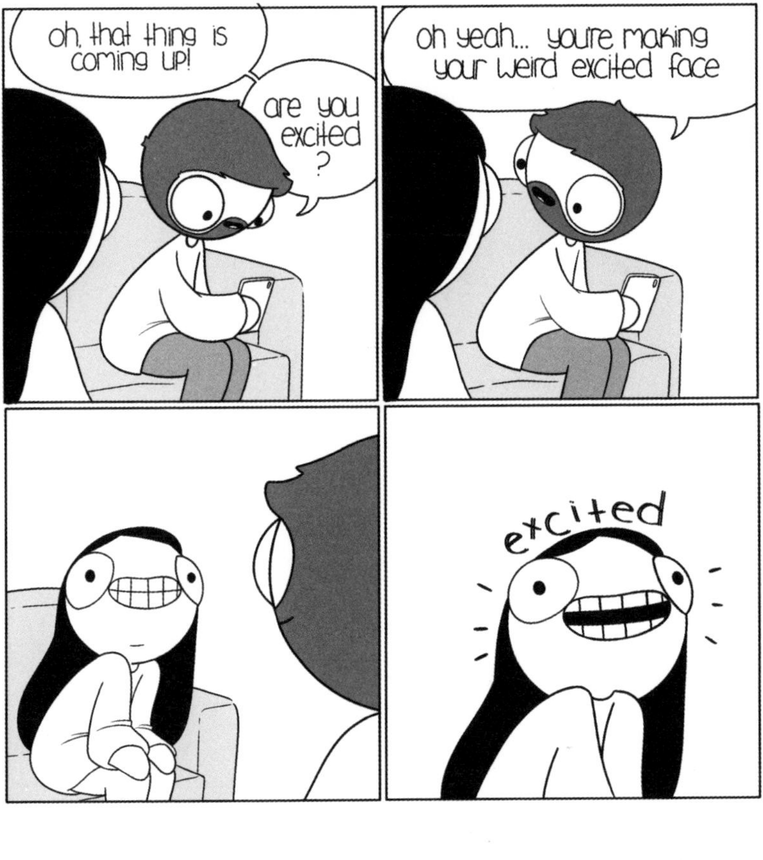
oh, that thing is coming up!
are you excited ?
oh yeah... you're making your weird excited face
excited

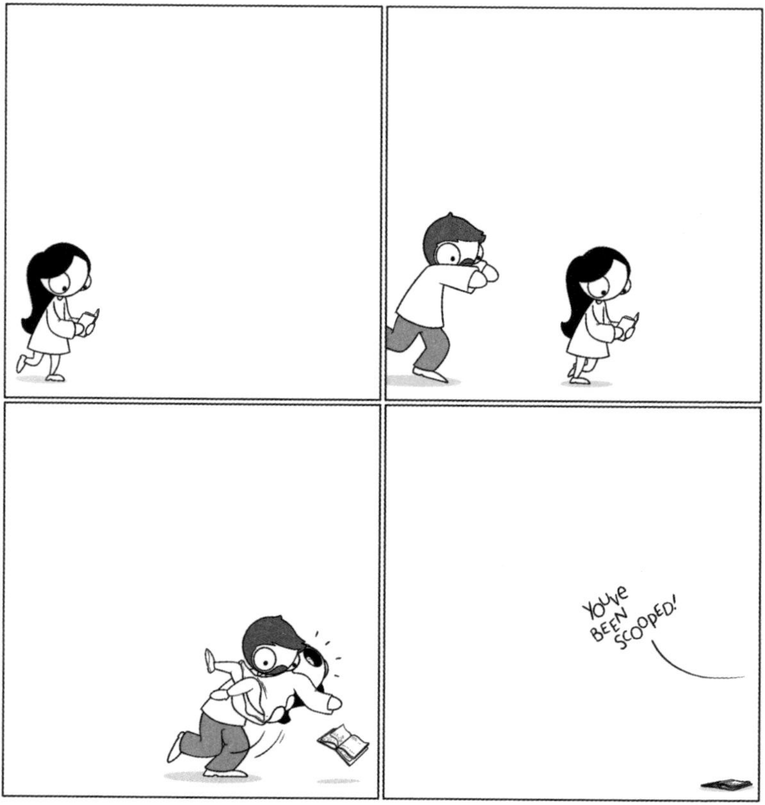
YOU'VE BEEN SCOOPED!

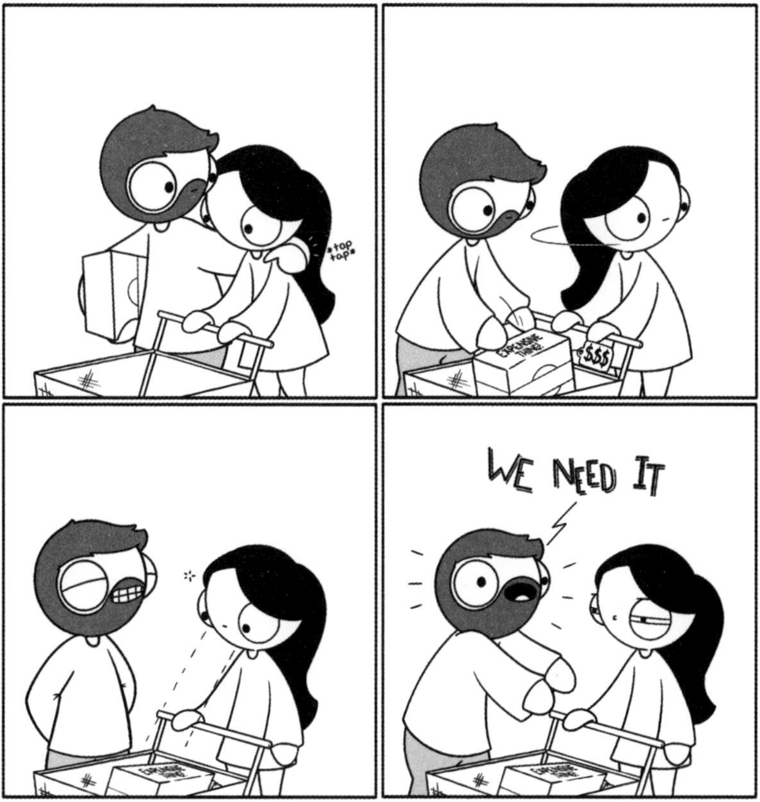
*tap tap*
EXPENSIVE THING
$$$
WE NEED IT

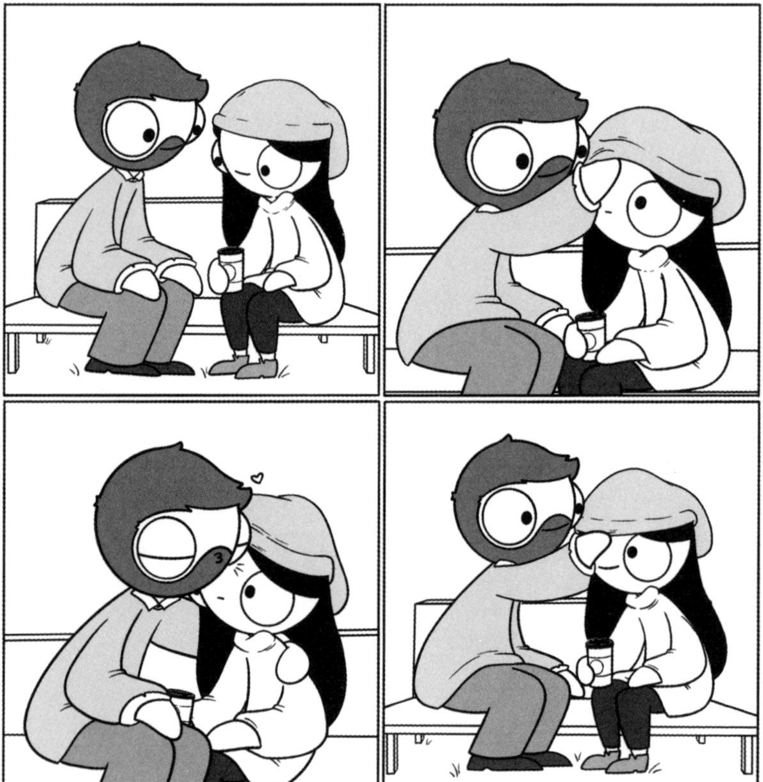

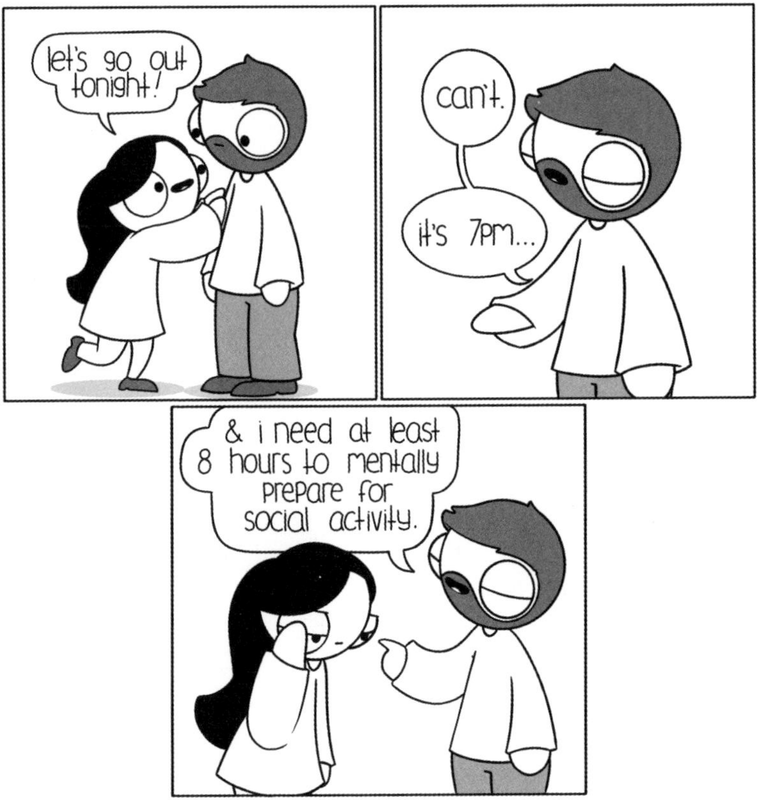
let's go out tonight!
can't.
it's 7pm...
& i need at least 8 hours to mentally prepare for social activity.

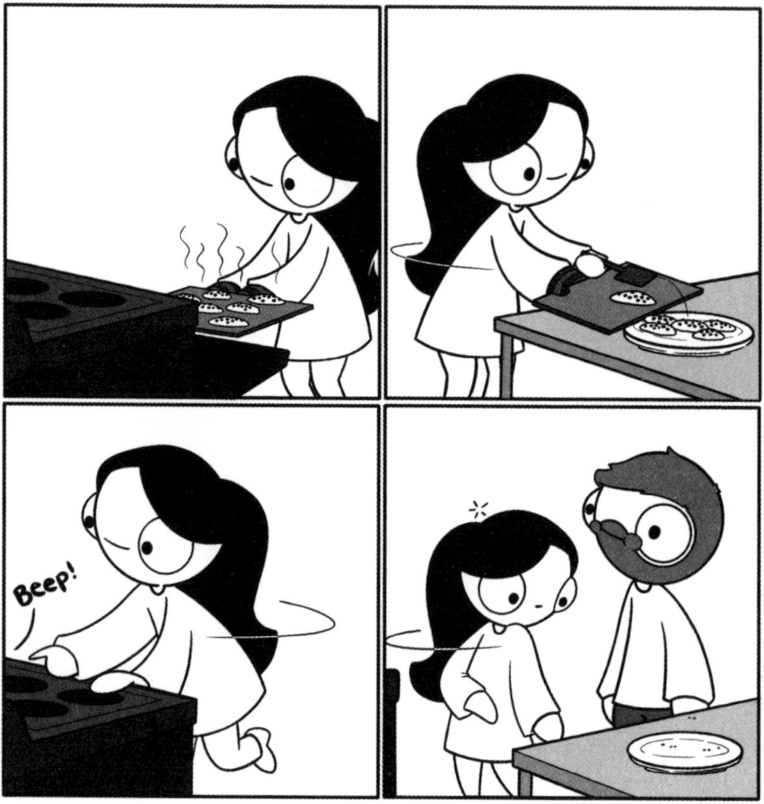
Beep!

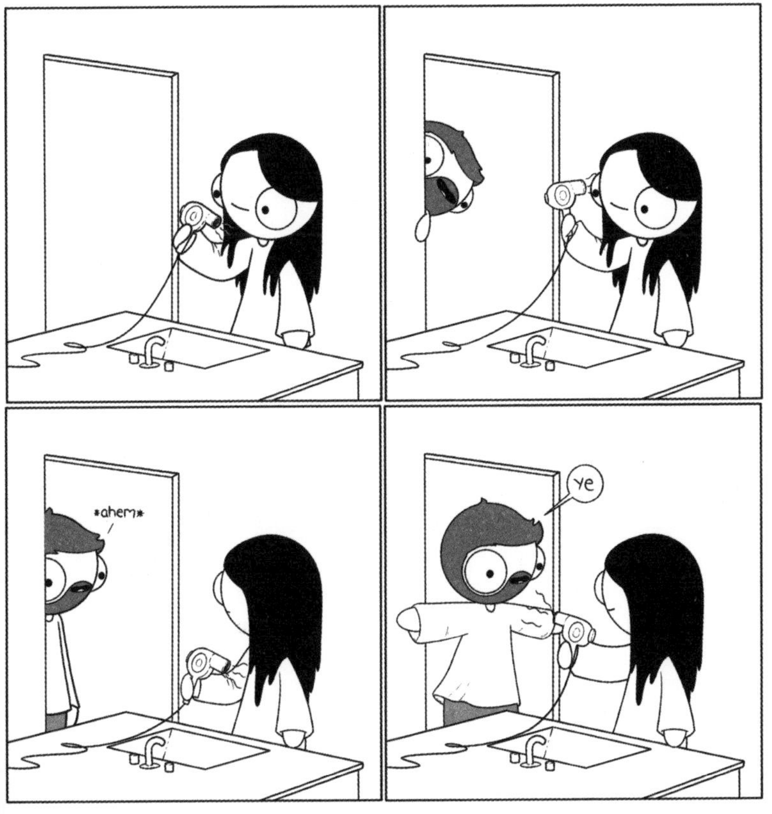
*ahem*
ye

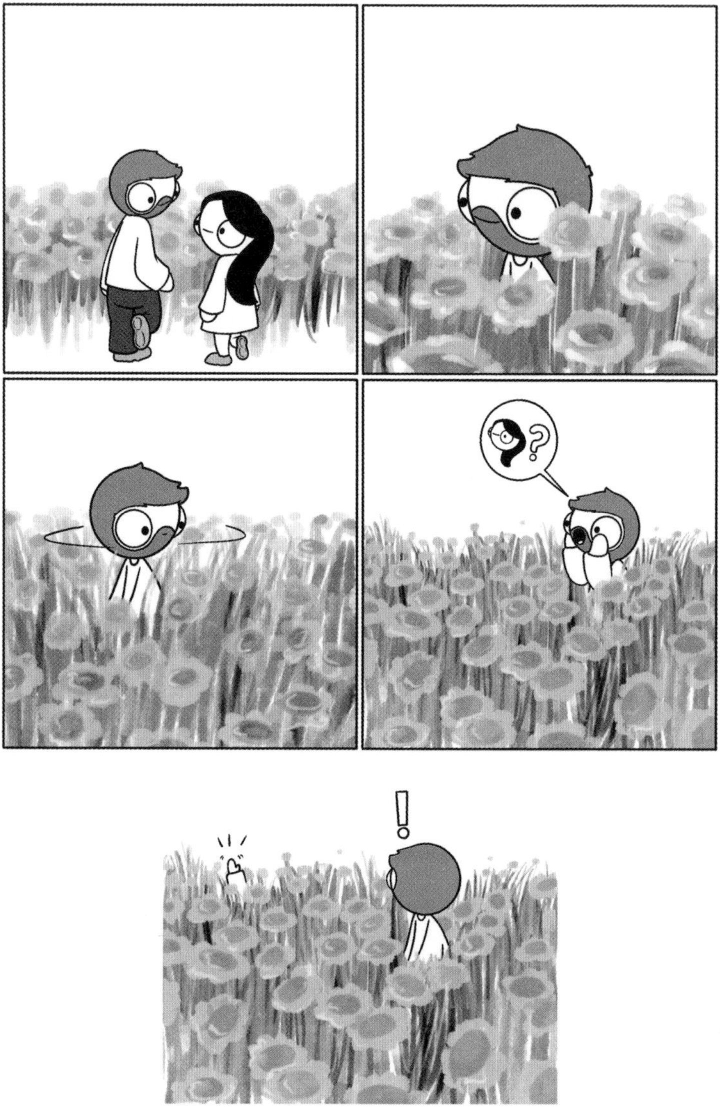

**Catana Chetwynd** is a self-taught traditional artist and the enthusiastic author of *Catana Comics*. She grew up in Saratoga Springs, New York, where she spent her time creating art and pursuing an education in psychology until accidentally stumbling into the world of comics. Not only is her fiancé, John, the daily inspiration for her drawings, but he was also the one who suggested a comic series about their relationship in the first place. Thanks to his idea and his inspiring daily antics, Catana was able to pursue her childhood dream of being a cartoonist. She currently lives on the East Coast with John and their tiny, angry dog, Murph.

Andrews McMeel Publishing
a division of Andrews McMeel Universal
1130 Walnut Street, Kansas City, Missouri 64106

www.andrewsmcmeel.com

21 22 23 24 25 SDB 10 9 8 7 6 5 4 3 2 1

ISBN: 978-1-5248-6471-2

Library of Congress Control Number: 2020942723

Editor: Patty Rice
Art Director/Designer: Holly Swayne
Production Editor: Amy Strassner
Production Manager: Tamara Haus